40 Weapons of War : A Devotional for Writers

Reggi Broach

Published by Defender Christian Publications, 2023.

Published by Defender Christian Publications
ISBN (Print): 978-1-950038-23-7
ISBN (Ebook): 978-1-950038-24-4
Unless otherwise noted, all scripture references are referenced from the New International Version (NIV), Biblica, 2011.

Cover Design: Reggi Broach
Cover Photo Credit: Ron Broach

Table of Contents

In Loving Memory of E. Grace Wilson

Introduction

The weapons we fight with are not the weapons of the world. On the contrary, they have divine power to demolish strongholds.
2 Corinthians 10:4

IN 1839, ENGLISH AUTHOR Edward Bulwer-Lytton penned the adage, "The pen is mightier than the sword." In a certain arena, the adage is true. Words are powerful and the Bible has a lot to say about our words. Our words can lift up or tear down. As Christians, our words should reflect the Word of God.

Ephesians 6:17 tells us that the sword of the Spirit is the "word of God." We as Christians are to be in the world, but not of the world. We don't fight like the world fights. Our battles are spiritual battles, and we need spiritual weapons. Hebrews tells us that the word of God is sharper than any double-edged sword.

When I originally felt called to write this devotional, I thought, sure, I could write an inspirational book targeting writers. I figured about thirty days, but then God asked me to make it forty days. Well, after a very brief argument, God won. The first inspirational nugget I would like to give you is, don't argue with God. God is not the enemy and if he asks something of us, he has a reason for it—and the means to accomplish it. The Lord will provide, and so he did. He gave me the additional devotional material.

As Christians, we are at war with evil and as writers, words are our weapons. My goal with this devotional is to address the struggles we face as writers that are unique to our station in life. I want you to have weapons in your war against the enemies of the kingdom of God. The goal of this devotional is to give writers Forty Weapons of War.

Each devotional contains a scripture to read, pray, and meditate on. You might even consider memorizing the scripture. I've related the scriptures to writers in particular. At the end, I've placed a song recommendation that draws everything together and a brief prayer to close out the thought. By all means, feel free to pray further than the written prayer. Use this devotional however God calls you to use it. Draw your weapon. Let's go to war!

SONG: *Battle Belongs* by Phil Wickham

PRAYER: Psalm 19:14 May these words of my mouth and this meditation of my heart be pleasing in your sight, Lord, my Rock and my Redeemer.

Pray First

"The royal administrators, prefects, satraps, advisers and governors have all agreed that the king should issue an edict and enforce the decree that anyone who prays to any god or human being during the next thirty days, except to you, Your Majesty, shall be thrown into the lions' den...So King Darius put the decree in writing. Now when Daniel learned that the decree had been published, he went home to his upstairs room where the windows opened toward Jerusalem. Three times a day he got down on his knees and prayed, giving thanks to his God, just as he had done before.
Daniel 6:7, 9-10

HOW MANY TIMES DO WE as individuals run into a problem or situation and the first thing we try to do is fix it? [Raises hand] I do.

We had a prayer event at church one year and the church handed out those stretchy rubber bracelets with the words "Pray First" on it. I gladly took one and I wear it every chance I get as a reminder to take things to God first, not as a last resort.

Daniel had the right idea. He had a habit of prayer, but when King Darius issued his edict to stop praying, what is the first thing Daniel did? He prayed—he went straight to God because it was his habit or custom and he didn't stop because of the potential consequences—even when the consequence promised was death.

Writing can be scary. We all ask, "Is what I write going to appeal to an audience?" or, "Did I say everything the best way possible?" The answer to that is likely going to be no because you'll always think, "Oh,

I should have said..." Does that mean don't write? Again, no. What if someone hates what I wrote? Someone will, but not everyone will. What if nobody buys my book? That's always a possibility. There are lots of reasons to stop writing or to never start. The only thing we can do is go to God about it.

We may be in the habit of morning or evening prayers, prayers before meals, prayer in church, but do we go to God before we write? Do we ask for his blessing and guidance in what we write? There are many types of writers across the planet. People who write fiction, non-fiction, devotionals, educational material, testimonials, sermons, and more.

Should you pray before writing a textbook on mitochondrial DNA or a cookbook? Is prayer any more or less important because what you are writing about is fact or fiction? I might not have quite the same passion for writing a non-fiction textbook as I do about writing fiction, but praying over a project is always a plus. God tells us to "pray without ceasing" (I Thessalonians 5:17 NKJV) and to put him first in our lives. Leave the outcome in his hands. Daniel ended up in a lion's den. Shadrach, Meshach, and Abednego were thrown into a fiery furnace. The apostles were executed or imprisoned. Pray and ask God for his guidance. Ask him to cover you and your work with his blessing and leave the consequences to him. You never know how your writing might impact someone's life. I decided a long time ago that if my life is the only one God changed by my writing, that was enough for me.

SONG: *What a Friend We Have in Jesus* by Paul Baloche

PRAYER: Heavenly Father, teach me to come to you first and leave the rest in your hands.

Be Still

God is our refuge and strength, an ever-present help in trouble. Therefore we will not fear, though the earth give way and the mountains fall into the heart of the sea, though its waters roar and foam and the mountains quake with their surging. There is a river whose streams make glad the city of God, the holy place where the Most High dwells. God is within her, she will not fall; God will help her at break of day. Nations are in uproar, kingdoms fall; he lifts his voice, the earth melts. The Lord Almighty is with us; the God of Jacob is our fortress. Come and see what the Lord has done, the desolations he has brought on the earth. He makes wars cease to the ends of the earth. He breaks the bow and shatters the spear; he burns the shields with fire. He says, "Be still, and know that I am God; I will be exalted among the nations, I will be exalted in the earth."

Psalm 46:1-10

IN TIMES OF STRESS and anxiety, it's easy to be overwhelmed. It can make focus nearly impossible. Our entire world may be falling apart because of lost jobs, new babies, death of friends or family, betrayal of a loved one, a frightening diagnosis, and many other possibilities—perhaps all of them at once. This entire planet can and will end up in ruins, but we have hope and options available to us.

The Psalmist tells us that the city of God will NOT fall. God is with us. The God of Jacob is our fortress, our refuge, our help in times of trouble. A fortress is a stationary place with walls of protection around it. It's not an army protecting our escape, it is the place we escape to, a safe place.

In Exodus, when the children of Israel were led out of Egypt, Pharaoh chased after them. The Israelites were ready to run although they were limited in where they could run to because they had a sea before them and Pharaoh's army behind them. Moses told them the Lord would fight for them and all they had to do was to be still.

How many times, when things go wrong, do we run around trying to fix them? Do we remember to commit our struggles to God? When our world starts falling apart, it's time to stop running and start praying. When we enter our refuge, our fortress provided by Almighty God, we need to be still and see his glory and help in our time of trouble. The Psalmist invites us to see what the Lord has done. When we get out of God's way, God will be exalted. *You* will know that he is God and *the world* will know that he is God.

There is a time to take our hands off the steering wheel and let God take us where he wants us to go. Many times I have been in a hurry to leave the house and can't find something very important, like car keys. In the scramble to get the kids ready and into the car, the diaper bag, and whatever else I needed, I can't find my keys, or one of the kids has lost a shoe and time is ticking to get to our destination. I can look in the same place three times, but do you know when and where I find my lost item? When I stop, pray, and take a deep breath. Where do I usually find the lost item? The place I already looked three times.

In those circumstances, I rest in the knowledge that God will give me what I need at the right time. Was the missing item hidden because of a potential accident on the interstate? Maybe. Was it a reminder to focus on him for that day? Maybe. Losing one's keys is such a minor crisis in the grander scheme of things, but it often starts my day with a dose of thankfulness. It pushes me to take that moment and stand in God's presence, and recognize his power and greatness.

God doesn't want us running in circles, crying, or throwing a tantrum when things go wrong. He wants us to watch him work. He would love to see us smile at the wondrous works he performs for us.

Is there a loved one that makes you smile when he or she walks into a room? Do *we* smile when God enters the room or we enter *his presence*? Do you think he smiles when we enter his presence? Sometimes I can feel him smiling at me, but if my thoughts are clouded with worries, doubts, and fears, I can miss that smile.

God is a miracle worker, a loving father, and many more things. Be still and see everything that you can. You don't want to miss anything.

SONG: *Into the Sea (It's Gonna Be Okay)* by Tasha Layton

PRAYER: Jesus, thank you for all the wondrous things you have done for us. Help us be still and see all the things we've been missing.

Listening for God's Voice

The Lord said, "Go out and stand on the mountain in the presence of the Lord, for the Lord is about to pass by."
Then a great and powerful wind tore the mountains apart and shattered the rocks before the Lord, but the Lord was not in the wind. After the wind there was an earthquake, but the Lord was not in the earthquake. After the earthquake came a fire, but the Lord was not in the fire. And after the fire came a gentle whisper. When Elijah heard it, he pulled his cloak over his face and went out and stood at the mouth of the cave.
Then a voice said to him, "What are you doing here, Elijah?"
I Kings 19:11-13

AS CHRISTIANS, WE TALK about having a personal relationship with Jesus. We work on our prayer lives by reading books on prayer, following the newest prayer trend, or the advice of Godly Christians. Our prayers include an offering of praise, thanksgiving, and a long list of problems to be solved. We close with another prayer of thanks for the answers to our prayers that haven't yet manifested themselves. There's nothing specifically wrong with that except we often forget to listen for God's voice.

The key word to look at here is "relationship." We have relationships with friends, family, coworkers, etc. The dynamics of each relationship are different. We aren't going to have the same levels of intimacy even among family members. There are some things we would discuss with our spouse that we wouldn't with our parents or siblings.

If we stopped talking to any of those we have relationships with, the relationship starts to dissolve. It doesn't necessarily disappear, but it affects us less and less. There are friends that I have known for over forty years that I haven't spoken to in several years. If I ran into my friend at the store, I would be glad to hug them and spend as long as I could catching up on their lives. They're still my friend, but except for the memories I have with them, we don't have much of a relationship. They don't have much of an impact on my daily life.

The same is true of God. If we don't spend time with him, his impact on our lives decreases. How do we have a relationship with someone we can't see and aren't even sure we hear? Have you ever had random ideas or thoughts pop into your head? According to Freud's psychoanalytic theory, there are three distinct elements that affect our actions, the id, the ego, and the superego. The superego is often illustrated as the good angel on our shoulder telling us what is right and wrong. The id is the bad angel on the opposite shoulder telling us to give in to our desires. The ego is the man in the middle who has to choose which voice to listen to. Satan would certainly prefer that we listen to his voice or that of the id. He prefers that we listen to any voice but God's. So how do we identify God's voice from our own desires or Satan's?

God uses a variety of methods to speak to us. He walked in the garden with Adam and Eve in the cool of the day to talk to them. He spoke to Moses through the burning bush. He used judges, prophets, and other methods. God spoke to John and several prophets through dreams and visions. Messengers came to Abram, Lot, and Mary.

In I Kings, Elijah was weary and dejected. He had been the instrument God had used to demonstrate God's will for the Israelites. He spoke God's words of warning and prophecy to King Ahab, had slain the prophets of Baal, and shown great zeal for the Lord. Elijah knew God's power. God's the one who sent the fire down on Elijah's sacrifice, sent the drought and the deluge that ended the drought.

Surely Elijah would expect for such a powerful God to be heard in a mighty wind, a quake that shook the earth, or a fire, like Moses' burning bush or the flames that consumed his sacrifice? Elijah was waiting and listening for God's voice and heard it as the still small voice.

The first time we meet someone, we may not learn their voice, but the more time we spend with them, the more likely we are to recognize their voice. Have you ever been in a store or restaurant and hear a voice that you recognized? If we don't practice listening for God's voice, we won't hear it. Life can get very busy and hectic and sometimes we miss it when he speaks.

As mentioned earlier, God can speak to us in several ways. There have been many times when I have been troubled and praying about a particular matter and God put a particular song on the radio that dealt with my pain. Ah! But that's just a coincidence, right? If you dismiss it as such, then you have not heard from God. He spoke, but you weren't listening. God can speak through coincidences, impressions, audible words, quiet whispers, scripture, and other methods. We learn to hear him through expecting to hear from him. We weigh those thoughts and impressions against scripture.

If you were to use the open the scripture and point to a verse method of trying to learn God's will for your life, you might go horribly awry. Genesis 22:10 says, "Then he reached out his hand and took the knife to slay his son." James 1:22(NKJV) says, "But be doers of the word, and not hearers only, deceiving yourselves." Well, this isn't going anyplace good, is it?

There are times when I have been writing, and a song would come on that so wonderfully represented the story I was writing, I was amazed. I thought, "Wow, this artist and I must be on the same wavelength." That wasn't what was happening. We were both serving the same God. We both had a relationship with the same Creator.

If we want to serve God and receive his truth, we can't take scripture out of context, and we can't pick and choose which scriptures to accept. Acts 13:22 tells us that God called David a man after his own heart. There is an underlying theme in the entirety of scripture that shows us God's heart. If we want to hear from God, we have to be willing to hear what he says, even if it disagrees with what we want. We have to be open to him and be actively listening for his voice. Put aside any hindrances, get away from distractions, and pray expecting God to speak to you.

David was a simple shepherd and the youngest in a house full of fine young men. Moses had a speech impediment and a murder charge hanging over his head. Paul was fervent about killing Christians. God spoke to the nobodies and the somebodies. Matthew 11:15, Matthew 13:9, Mark 4:9 & 23, Luke 8:8, and Luke 14:35 say, "Whoever has ears, let them hear." He said it at least six times. Were you listening?

FOR MORE ON THIS TOPIC, I recommend *Hearing God* by Dallas Willard.

SONG: *God Speaking* by Mandisa

PRAYER: Speak, Lord, your servant is listening.

Doubt

Now the serpent was more crafty than any of the wild animals the Lord God had made. he said to the woman, "Did God really say, 'You must not eat from any tree in the garden'?"
Genesis 3:1

WHEN EVE WAS IN THE garden of Eden, she wasn't familiar with doubt, temptation, or fear. God walking through the garden in the cool of the day was the norm. She had a garden where she had more than enough to eat and a wide variety of options. God had provided her with everything she needed. She had no reason to doubt him.

Thomas earned a reputation for doubt. His doubt carried him to a point of being in denial. His hopes of Jesus being the Messiah were crushed when Jesus died. He wasn't going to even consider that Christ was alive unless he saw it for himself. His denial, doubts, and fear choked the hope and joy the other disciples were trying to share with him. He didn't want to be let down again. If the Sanhedrin had Jesus killed, would they come after him next? Would he ever be allowed in the temple or in the synagogues again? If Jesus wasn't the path to salvation, his Jewish roots were all he had left and if that was no longer available to him, was he condemned to a life without God? We can only speculate what he might have been thinking. His doubts surely piled up until he succumbed to fear and denial.

Peter was walking on the water toward Jesus. He walked far enough to be out of reach of the boat, but not close enough to reach Jesus yet. Doubt slipped in and took over and he lost his footing on the waves.

Doubt destabilizes you. It is a weapon of the enemy. When doubts start to arise, it's time to fight back. Identify your questions and hesitations for what they are. Pray for God's guidance and protection, believe he will give it, then move forward again.

When I first started writing, I had no doubt that it was an answer to prayer. My doubts came when I started questioning whether I was "called" to be a writer. I believed I was, but doubts kept hounding me and the question entered my mind, "Did God really say...?" I recognized that phrase. Those were the words the serpent spoke to Eve in the garden. Today, that question is settled in my mind. The whispers still try to gain a foothold in my mind, but I know it is not my Father's voice that I hear.

The second battle that I face where doubt is concerned in my writing career is whether what I write is acceptable. This battle is like a game of "Whack-a-mole." First, one pops its head up, then another, and another, then two at once. Is this scene too violent? Is it violent enough? Am I saying this in a way that is theologically sound despite the fact that it's fiction? Would God be pleased with this? Are my stories worth reading?

On the other side of the coin, what if I can't get a publisher to pick up my story? What if they want me to change what I've written? What if this genre isn't selling in the current market? What if someone gave me a bad review?—maybe I shouldn't be a writer.

Doubt leads to worry, which leads to fear. Doubt can also lead to confusion. Eve saw the bountiful garden around her but focused on the one thing she didn't fully understand and began to doubt God. Was God denying her something or hiding something from her? She had access to everything else in the garden. Why not this? Thomas saw Jesus and Peter walking on the water. He saw the dead raised. He was there when the five thousand were fed. Thomas had evidence of God's power, but he doubted. He became afraid to believe even when his friends testified to him that Jesus was alive.

When we lose focus, it's unclear whether we should stay on the course we are on, or choose another path. The goals ahead of us become fuzzy.

Faith is the absence of doubt. In Matthew 21:21 Jesus says, "Truly I tell you, if you have faith and do not doubt, not only can you do what was done to the fig tree, but also you can say to this mountain, 'Go, throw yourself into the sea,' and it will be done."

Doubt is the fear that things which haven't happened, might happen. Faith is believing things that haven't happened yet, will. Doubt causes anxiety where faith brings peace and comfort.

James 1:5-8 says,

"If any of you lacks wisdom, you should ask God, who gives generously to all without finding fault, and it will be given to you. But when you ask, you must believe and not doubt, because the one who doubts is like a wave of the sea, blown and tossed by the wind. That person should not expect to receive anything from the Lord. Such a person is double-minded and unstable in all they do."

FIGHT DOUBT WITH FAITH. God doesn't want us to doubt him or his Word, even the word he gives to us on a personal level. God has been faithful to us. He was faithful to all of humanity. When man fell in the garden, he promised to redeem us and thousands of years later, our savior was born, died, and rose again. He promised Abraham a son and to make his descendants as numerous as the stars in the sky. Today, we cannot count Abraham's descendants. Doubt is a hindrance to God's will in our lives.

God chose people who were nothing special, even people that were hated. Abraham was nothing until God called him. Moses was a murderer, David was a teenager and a shepherd, the disciples were fishermen, and other less desirables. Who am I that God would choose me?

Put God in front of you and always seek to honor him and your faith will be rewarded.

SONG: *Even If* by MercyMe

PRAYER: Father, give us the faith that surpasses the grain of mustard seed.

Best or Less?

Study to shew thyself approved unto God, a workman that needeth not to be ashamed, rightly dividing the word of truth.
2 Timothy 2:15 (KJV)

AS WRITERS, WE DEAL with many things. If we write non-fiction, depending on the nature of what we write, we can deal with factual events and/or real life emotions. We also deal with God's truth. As writers of fiction, what we write reflects genuine emotions, actual conflicts, and real truth about God and his nature.

No matter what we write, God calls us to present him with our best. How do we accomplish that? Prayer should always be the first step. Study should be the next step. What should you study? Good question. Writers deal with so many things. Studying God's Word is a good place to start. As we write, our understanding of God and the scriptures is reflected. If we don't understand who God is and why he does what he does, we can mislead our readers. Scripture is the first thing you want to study.

The next thing you want to do is to have an understanding of what you are writing about. When you write fiction, you often create an entire world that doesn't exist on any map or timeline. How do you study something that isn't real? You don't, but you can be consistent with the rules you create. The things you might need to study are the parts that are real. For example, when writing historical fiction, you need to know the time period you're writing about. Study the historical events and technology of the period.

Not cutting corners on an imaginary world, in an imaginary time, with invented people may not seem important, but it is. Putting less than your best effort into the technical aspects can distract the reader from any Biblical truths you are trying to convey. God created you in his own image. You are a representation of him and your characters are a reflection of you.

Writers are always doing research. What else do we need to do to show ourselves as approved and a worker who doesn't need to be ashamed? Don't skimp on the other aspects of publishing. Use a good editor and follow the guidelines for creating a cover that fits the industry standards for your genre. Learn what font you should use. If you don't know how to do something, either learn it yourself or hire someone to do it for you.

Our books, stories, poems, songs, or sermons are an offering to God and for his glory. If you stood in front of God with your creation, would you be eager for him to see it, or would you try to hide it? Even if you think it isn't very good, did you do your best on it? Are you giving him your best effort, or whatever is left over at the end of the day?

God is worthy of far more than the best we could ever offer him. Do you really want to give him your mediocrity? Not everyone is an award-winning author, but that doesn't mean don't write.

We should give all that we have like the widow giving her two mites. Her offering was smaller than the offerings given by others, but she gave all that she had. She gave because she loved God. Your offering reveals what's in your heart.

SONG: *Worthy Of It All* as performed by Matt Redman

PRAYER: Jesus, remind us that our work is a sacrifice of praise and glory to your name.

A Noble Theme

My heart is stirred by a noble theme as I recite my verses for the king; my tongue is the pen of a skillful writer.
Psalm 45:1

IF I WON A MILLION dollars, I would certainly be excited, and I would have to tell somebody about it. When someone is passionate about something, they can't wait to share it. Over the years, I have been passionate about many things; homeschooling, the Civil Air Patrol, seeing God's hand at work, and other things.

When the realization of what Christ did for me and for everyone hits home, I am astounded, and I want to share that. I remember thinking about the story of creation and realizing God knew before he ever created man what Adam and Eve would do in that garden, and what terrible price would have to be paid. Jesus knew what these two people would cost him, but created them anyway. He created all of us knowing how we would turn out, and about the joys and sorrows we would bring him. The joy must surely outweigh the sorrows.

I'm not much of an evangelist. Nevertheless, I am passionate about what God has done for me and the things he has done in my life. I'm not afraid to speak in front of others, but my brain doesn't verbalize things very well. My tongue, unlike the psalmist above, is not the pen of a skillful writer. I am a writer with a reasonable amount of skill and a noble verse stirs my heart. The verse I write is for my King, the King of all Kings.

Whether I write a devotional like this one, a poem, an autobiography about God's work in my life, or a work of fiction, my heart seeks to sing the praises of my God and profess my love for him. Even if what I am writing doesn't specifically point to God, my heart rejoices that he gave me a way to express the things that matter in my life.

We can be excited about a lot of things, like our favorite sports team winning the championship game, our baby saying its first word, or our child making the honor roll. The noble theme that stirs our hearts should revolve around the greatness of God. He should be what motivates our entire life.

SONG: *Good Feeling* by Austin French

PRAYER: Thank you, Heavenly Father, for sending your Son, Jesus, to save us from our sins and for being the theme that stirs our hearts.

Write what God Tells You

"This is what the Lord, the God of Israel, says: 'Write in a book all the words I have spoken to you.
Jeremiah 30:2

GOD INSTRUCTED SEVERAL people to write his messages. Moses wrote laws, covenants, historical documents, and lists. He instructed the children of Israel to write the Lord's statutes on their door frames and gates. Besides Jeremiah and Moses, the prophets Ezekiel and Habakkuk were commanded to write. Paul gave messages to the early churches using the method of writing. David wrote Psalms out of pain, sorrow, frustration, joy, and love. Did these men know they were writing the things that we now hold in such high esteem and consider to be the Divinely inspired Word of God? Some were writing in obedience to God and some wrote from their hearts. Today, they bear equal weight as the Word of God.

Sometimes God commands writing, and sometimes writing is the preferred method of conveying a message. It may be a chosen method, a necessity, a convenience, or a command. Some people have a natural talent for writing, and others work to be skilled at it.

God gave Moses and the prophets the task of writing, and his message has a purpose. God may not use our works the same way he uses what Jeremiah wrote, but he still has a purpose for what we write. Whether we are writing fiction, educational material, inspirational books, or research grants, God calls us to do all things for his glory.

In Jeremiah chapter thirty, God explains to the Kingdom of Judah what was about to happen and why. He promises his children that he isn't abandoning them or leaving them without hope.

Jeremiah's writings were not well received. In chapter thirty-six, one of his messages was read to the King of Judah. Every time the King heard something he didn't like, the King cut out the portion of the scroll and threw it into the fire until the entire scroll was burned. Jeremiah wasn't writing to please the people or the King. He was writing because God commanded it. Jeremiah and his scribe went into hiding after writing the scroll and God had to hide them from the King.

Several years ago, I was about to undergo a routine medical procedure and, being a nurse; I knew what things could happen to me. I struggled and worried and fretted. God told me to write down everything I was worried about, so I did. I thought he was just having me do a therapeutic journal writing. That wasn't quite the case. After I was done, he told me to point to the worries on my list that I thought he couldn't handle. Boy, did I feel dumb. There wasn't a problem on that page that he couldn't handle.

He instructed me to write, but what I wrote in that journal was not God breathed. I've read many inspirational or devotional type books I believe God inspired and blessed, but they do not carry the weight of scripture.

When God tells us to do something, he has a reason. To disobey can bear consequences, some smaller and some larger. We may miss a blessing, someone else may miss a blessing, Jonah's great fish may pay us a visit, or worse.

Jeremiah wrote what God told him to, but the message was rejected by the King. Jeremiah probably suffered feelings of personal rejection because of the King's reaction. Was he hurting for himself, the children of Israel, or was he sorrowful because the God he loved was being rejected? He was likely feeling all those things to some degree. How do we react when our works are rejected, our reviews are bad, or our sales are down?

Jesus told his disciples that they would be hated because the world hates him. The world doesn't want to hear what God has to say or what we have to say about God.

Naturally, we want our writing to be well-received. Although that may not always happen, we need to write to please God more than mankind. If you write a Godly work and the world dislikes or despises you for it, you're in good company. The world hated Jesus and a good many of the prophets. There are a lot of reasons to not write. What if nobody likes my writing? What if I'm not successful? What if I don't do it well? What if that isn't what God really wants? What if...?

On the other hand, what if we don't write and someone misses God's blessing? What if we don't write and we miss God's blessing in our own lives? What if the story we could write strikes a chord in another's life? The joys, sorrows, and struggles we put into even an imaginary world could help one person see they aren't alone in their own struggles. If writing is God's plan for your life, don't rob God, yourself, or others by choosing not to write.

SONG: *Write Your Story* by Francesca Battistelli

PRAYER: Father, give me the courage to write and may my writing be pleasing in your sight, Oh God.

Called to Write?

Nevertheless, each person should live as a believer in whatever situation the Lord has assigned to them, just as God has called them. This is the rule I lay down in all the churches.
I Corinthians 7:17

IN I CORINTHIANS 7:17, Paul says we should live as believers in whatever situation the Lord has assigned to us. So, are you called to write?

I Corinthians 12 talks about the spiritual gifts. Paul lists these gifts according to priority. Writers didn't exactly make the list of Spiritual Gifts, or did they? In the first verse listed, Paul says in whatever situation (nothing specific is mentioned) but he follows with the phrase "just as God called them."

Some people are called to a profession, while others use a profession to pay the bills while they serve the Lord. How many are "Called" to be garbage collectors, truck drivers, wait staff, musicians, customer service representatives, cashiers, mechanics, medical personnel, and many others? None of the careers mentioned are typically what you would consider a Divine calling. There are some situations where God does call a person to those careers. How do we know the difference between callings and jobs that are there just to pay the bills? For example, the apostle Paul was a tentmaker. It was a skill that he used to support his physical needs, but it was not his calling. His calling was to preach the gospel.

What does it mean to be called? God calls us by putting a burden in our hearts or minds, a burning desire, or a straight up command. Jonah was commanded to go to Nineveh. Obviously, Jonah did not have a burden or burning desire to go to Nineveh. David had a burning desire to serve the Lord and honor him. His desire propelled him to build a temple for God, but God stopped him because of the amount of blood on his hands. Nehemiah was called by a burning desire to rebuild the walls around Jerusalem. God called Cyrus, King of Persia, to build a temple for God in Jerusalem. Cyrus wasn't one of the children of Israel, but God still called him.

God called some of his prophets, apostles, and Kings to write certain messages. King David wrote his Psalms out of his creative ability and his passion for God. To our knowledge, God didn't command David to write, but he was called to write out of his love, pain, and dependence on God.

Have you ever had a particular message on your heart and mind, then you hear a song on the radio that echoes it, and a pastor or Bible study repeats it? I've had that happen and thought, "Wow, we must be a lot alike to be thinking the same things." I finally came to realize it isn't so much that I have things in common with a particular singer or pastor, but that we know the same Jesus who is at the source of those thoughts.

People share their love for the Lord through the things they do and the skills they have. There's a man that has a talent for woodworking. He builds little footstools for the shorter members of his church congregation as well as carving birds and other creative endeavors. He ministers to people through his creations. Another may minister through doing yard work for the shut-ins or sick.

God sometimes specifically calls individuals to a task and sometimes he creates a person with a particular gift who gives out of the abundance of the heart. You may be called to write, or God may have gifted you with a talent or desire. Does that make what you do any more or less important? No, it doesn't.

Yes, you can be called to be a writer. Only you can say whether that is true in your own case. God called the prophets to do some pretty strange things in the old testament. The apostle Paul and King David's actions were out of love and zeal for the Lord. Whether your calling is a command or a burning desire isn't important, so long as you follow that calling. Is writing a Spiritual Gift? It can be. I can read or write a book that has nothing more than entertainment value or I can write or read a book to learn. Teaching is a Spiritual Gift. How many times have we read a science fiction book written many years ago and thought it was prophetic because we've seen the things written about come to pass? A writer could be a prophet and a prophet can be a writer.

Don't let yourself be talked out of writing or having a "call" to write if that's what God has spoken to you. Don't let others tell you that God doesn't call you to write steam punk, or fantasy, or anything else because it didn't make the list. God told Isaiah to run around naked (Isaiah 20:2), Hosea to marry a promiscuous woman (Hosea 1:2), and Ezekiel to eat a scroll (Ezekiel 3). He can call you to write a book.

In whatever situation you are in, obey what God calls you to do and do whatever you can to bring glory to his name.

SONG: *Soul on Fire* by Third Day

PRAYER: Jesus, let my love and zeal for you overflow into all that I do so that no one doubts it is you that I serve.

Educate

Not only was the Teacher wise, but he also imparted knowledge to the people. He pondered and searched out and set in order many proverbs. The Teacher searched to find just the right words, and what he wrote was upright and true.
Ecclesiastes 12:9-10

WHEN I WRITE, MY GOALS are to entertain, educate, and evangelize. God gave me the task of writing a variety of works, including fiction and nonfiction. Whichever one I write, the goals remain the same—although the focus may lean more heavily on one area than another. In my life, I lean heavily into teaching. As a safety officer in the Civil Air Patrol and my job was to educate participants on safe behavior and the rights and responsibilities of participants to stop unsafe activities. My husband and I homeschooled our children. As a nurse, patient education is a big part of my job.

In I Corinthians 12, Paul lists the spiritual gifts and teaching is the third one on the list. Education is a high priority in all aspects of life. As infants, our parents teach us to say new words and how to hold a spoon—as we grow, our education continues. Parents and church teachers teach us about right and wrong and how to love God. School teachers instruct us on reading, writing, history, science, and math.

Today, the internet provides us with an abundance of information from instructional videos, news articles, research, and much more. You can learn almost anything, but is what you are learning accurate? Can you trust the information or the sponsor?

In Ecclesiastes 12:10, it talks about the teacher looking for the right words. Education is multifaceted. A teacher may prefer method "A" of teaching, but the student may learn better through method "B."

When writing about a difficult concept, you are limited to the written word to teach. There are no visual demonstrations or activities. The words need to be concise, yet detailed enough to get the point across. Writing non-fiction bears the full weight of writing what is "upright and true." (Ecc 12:10)

Although works of fiction are about imaginary things, certain things need to be upright and true. Discounting God's nature or disparaging his nature as a *primary* theme in your writing leads the reader astray. Yes, there are people out there who do not believe or trust in God and they might write something that does those things. However, as Christians, we have a responsibility to educate the non-believer and not lead them astray. What you write doesn't have to even mention God, but it cannot mislead the reader into thinking God is something that he is not.

On the other side of the education coin is learning to be a better writer. If we are to be like the teacher in Ecclesiastes, we need to hone our skills and education. Granted, there are some gray areas in writing, but knowing the right ways and wrong ways helps you to know when you should step into and out of those gray areas.

Writers are typically very good at learning because they do lots of research. If you check their browser history, you're going to find lots of interesting topics like plants and their uses, when a particular invention was made, diagrams and names of ship layouts, the speed of a hurricane, theoretical questions such as the speed of an unladen African swallow, and more. We don't need to forget to enhance our learning about sentence structures, character development, and story arcs. We may have an awesome adventure and a fantastic moral to our story, but if the reader can't get past the lack of subject verb agreement or the haphazard manner that we push our characters through the story, the message is lost.

2 Timothy 2:15 (KJV) "Study to shew thyself approved unto God, a workman that needeth not to be ashamed, rightly dividing the word of truth."

To teach through writing, we need to know the truth about what we are saying and the best ways to say it. Jesus began learning early on and demonstrated his abilities by confounding the teachers in the temple at the age of twelve. He taught using different methods. He asked questions to challenge the listener to think. He told stories, preached sermons, and set the example for us to follow. He used miracles to prove he had power and authority. He praised those who had great faith and condemned those who doubted.

Education is an ongoing, forward journey. We need to learn all that we can so that we can teach all that we can. Speak the truth, teach the truth, and write the truth in love and wisdom. Jesus is the light of the world and as writers, we can and should use our writing to share that light in the best ways we can. Luke 6:40 says, "The student is not above the teacher, but everyone who is fully trained will be like their teacher."

To be a better teacher, we need to be teachable and have a humble heart. Be willing to learn and share what we've learned even through an imaginary world.

SONG: Hymns - *Tell Me the Story of Jesus* written by Fanny J. Crosby and *Open My Eyes, That I May See* written by Chas. H. Scott

PRAYER: Father, give me the heart and mind to learn all I can and teach all I can.

Lament

Joy is gone from our hearts; our dancing has turned to mourning. The crown has fallen from our head. Woe to us, for we have sinned! Because of this our hearts are faint, because of these things our eyes grow dim for Mount Zion, which lies desolate, with jackals prowling over it.
Lamentations 5:15-18

LIFE IS HARD. INJUSTICE and sin are prevalent in the world. The pain of loss and depression hurts. Many times we stick our fingers in our ears and hum as we pass by the ugliness in the world and our lives. Perhaps I should say that we turn on some praise music, watch a happy movie, or get lost in a "nice" fairy tale. If we stare too long at the darkness, we will lose the joy from our hearts and our dancing will turn to mourning.

This is escapism. Should we embrace or escape the darker side of life? For those suffering from depression and anxiety, escape is harder.

Ecclesiastes 3:4 tells us there is a time for weeping, laughing, mourning, and dancing. Wallowing in the abyss of depression, sadness, regret, and loss on a daily basis is not where you want to stay—however, pretending it doesn't exist is also not the best option.

To lament is to strongly express regret or sorrow, to wail and mourn loudly. Job loved his first ten children so much that he would offer sacrifices for them regularly. He knew about the sins of the heart. Even if his children didn't feel sorrow or regret, Job did.

Jeremiah was known as the weeping prophet because the sins of God's chosen people broke his heart. Jeremiah wept over the sins of all the children of Israel, not just those who were simply close blood relations. God called him to be a prophet to the nations.

Humans prefer to stay on the happy side of life with good reason—happy feels good. As Christians, we look at God, who is good, but don't look too closely at the God who is our judge and the one who disciplines us. Am I suggesting that all bad things are God's judgment? No. God is still a good God and his discipline is righteous and fair. He disciplines his children to teach them to behave better, as a good parent should.

God is merciful and we like to extol that particular virtue, but we forget what he is being merciful toward. God extends his mercy to sinners. Sinners range from the complacent sweet little old lady who never bothers to care about God and his plans to the villainous serial killer. We are all sinners. Jesus is the only one who has ever escaped that label.

When we look at the sin in the world and consider it—really consider it—it's heartbreaking. The way people treat each other. Looking at the news, there are children dying of starvation, murders in the streets, churches burning to the ground, and untold atrocities. Christians are martyred just for being Christian and daring to spread the gospel. If you dwell on it, it can overwhelm you with heartbreak.

As a writer, I have struggled with putting certain scenarios into my books, fearing they were too dark and ugly. It isn't because the scenarios are fiction, but because they are too real and my target audience is primarily Christian. To be honest, I've not written anything darker than the things that are found in scripture. If you look at the prophecies and the description of Christ's death on the cross, it is incredibly graphic.

Christians are often viewed as lambs, and with good reason. However, the analogy is often misapplied. While we are sheep and Jesus is our shepherd, we are also soldiers called to put on armor for a battle.

Satan is the enemy that we are battling against. It's great to sing our songs of worship and victory to help us get inspired for battle, but where is the righteous indignation about the injustices in the world? David didn't take on Goliath because the King offered a reward. David was angry that this uncircumcised Philistine would challenge God and his chosen people.

A writer who wants to overcome the injustice, and the pain, has to know and understand the pain. Writers have to convey the hearts and minds of their characters. Everyone has lost a loved one at some point and that's perhaps a little easier to convey, but to convey the disparity between humanity and our sin is the hardest. Humans justify themselves in their own eyes. Looking at one's self as being "not that bad" is easy to do.

To understand human depravity, we need to look at ourselves from God's perspective. When we see ourselves the way he sees us, we can't help but weep in sorrow over sin. Don't run from such a view, but face it. If your heart breaks over sin, you can convey that same sorrow to others. Approach God's throne, asking for the mercy none of us deserve. See the world as a world in need. Pray for the hearts of your family, your neighbors, your governmental leaders, your nation, and the world. Your efforts may change the world as well as enrich the depths of your writing.

SONGS: *O God Forgive Us* by for King & Country featuring KB and *Give Me Your Eyes by* Brandon Heath

PRAYER: Father, help us to see the world as you see it and love others the way you love them.

Evangelize

Therefore go and make disciples of all nations, baptizing them in the name of the Father and of the Son and of the Holy Spirit, and teaching them to obey everything I have commanded you. And surely I am with you always, to the very end of the age.
Matthew 28:19-20

JESUS COMMANDED HIS disciples to make disciples of others and that command extends to all believers. The first step to making disciples is to be a disciple. You can't teach, preach, or share what you don't know or have. Jesus didn't command all believers to be another Billy Graham, but we are all called to share the gospel with those around us. Since no two people are identical, and even identical twins have differences, each of us handles this command differently.

Writers are often introverts. How does an introvert make disciples? The first step is to be a disciple of Christ.

Being a disciple means we have to first be a student of the Word—to sit at Jesus' feet, learning and interacting with him. The scriptures tells us that if we draw closer to God, he will draw closer to us (James 4:8a). Research is a significant part of a writer's life. I grew up in the church and know my Bible very well. However, in writing about any single topic in this devotional, I often had a half-dozen browser tabs open to various sections of the Bible, researching things I supposedly know very well. Learning from scripture is an ongoing part of being a disciple.

Being a disciple goes beyond research and learning. There are some very learned people in this world that I wouldn't trust to give me spiritual advice. Knowledge may give you power, but only if you know how to use it. There's a story about a man who wanted to know God's will about some event in his life, so he opened his Bible and pointed to a scripture. It was the one stating that Judas went out and hanged himself (Matthew 27:5). He decided it was just a fluke, so he randomly opened it again and pointed to a second scripture which said, "go and do thou likewise." (Luke 10:37) The flustered man tried a third time and pointed to a scripture that said, "That thou doest, do quickly." You can know the scripture, but if you don't know the context or how to use it, it doesn't do you any good. You also have to know the author of the scripture.

The last part of today's scripture is a promise from Jesus that he will always be with us. When we are with someone, we may have periods of silence where both are busy with their own tasks, but they are together. In other situations, two people can interact while working together on a joint task. The same is true with Jesus. We may not be interacting openly, but he's still with us, interceding for us, and loving us. Other times, we need to have interactions, seeking his will for our lives and establishing a two-way relationship with him. This means, when we pray, he gets to talk too.

Evangelizing is one of my personal goals in writing. According to my Myers-Briggs evaluation, I am 53% Introvert. According to my Spiritual Gifts evaluation, evangelism is not where I scored well. How does an introverted non-evangelist evangelize?

Have you ever had an excited child grab your hand and pull you to something they've just discovered? After they show you that bug on a leaf, they have a thousand questions about it and if you don't know the answers, you'll be chasing those answers down yourself. You become a temporary disciple of a bug on a leaf.

When we get excited about something, it's hard to keep from sharing it in some way. Our faith and love for the Lord should permeate all that we do. Our writing should clearly reflect that and not detract from it. There are people who may not go near a Bible, but they might read an entertaining story. That story may cause them to ask questions and seek answers that only the Bible can speak to. If God can use our writing to draw souls to his Word, then that is awesome.

SONG: *Go Tell it on the Mountain* by various artists

PRAYER: Father, fill us up with your love to the point that we overflow onto those around us, drawing them to you.

Jesus is the Light

When Jesus spoke again to the people, he said, "I am the light of the world. Whoever follows me will never walk in darkness, but will have the light of life."
John 8:12

WHEN SIN ENTERED THE world, darkness shrouded humanity. It's interesting that the Bible says when Adam and Eve ate the forbidden fruit, their eyes were opened. They could see something that they had never seen before: spiritual darkness. We don't really know how long they were in the garden before the fall, but it seemed to be long enough that they had a routine. It was probably long enough for them to be comfortable and to have explored the entire garden tasting all the fruits and vegetables it offered. The serpent presented them with perhaps the only fruit they hadn't tried yet.

Adam and Eve were naked the entire time. They had seen each other, and it didn't bother them until the day they took the fruit and ate it. The knowledge of good and evil opened their eyes to spiritual darkness. They saw physical darkness on a daily basis with the rising and setting of the sun. This was a new darkness, the darkness marked by sin and death that would carry on to every generation. A darkness that has cursed us all. Spiritual darkness was already present in creation because Satan and a third of the angels in heaven had fallen into sin. Adam and Eve couldn't see it and weren't aware of it, just like they weren't aware of their own nakedness.

Adam and Eve knew God created them and the garden they lived in. They knew they could eat from any tree except the tree of knowledge of good and evil. They knew God told them the consequences of eating from the tree was death. They chose instead to reach for the forbidden knowledge, the desire to be like their creator, and the taste of something new.

Isaiah 9:2 says, "The people walking in darkness have seen a great light; on those living in the land of deep darkness a light has dawned." Jesus claimed that title. Sin brought death and darkness, but Christ brought light and life.

In John 3:16, Jesus explained that his mission was to save the world, at least those who chose to believe in him. His purpose wasn't to bring condemnation, but forgiveness to those who desired to have forgiveness. Whoever follows Jesus will have light to see. How many times have people justified their actions as being right simply because they want it to be right? People who justify their actions aren't looking for the light or forgiveness. They are satisfying themselves and continuing to walk in darkness.

After Jesus ascended into Heaven, the apostles were persecuted by the Sanhedrin. A Pharisee named Gamaliel wisely advised the Sanhedrin to leave the men alone. If what the disciples were doing was of human origin, it would eventually fade away, but if it was from God, there was no way to stop it. Whether Gamaliel was a secret follower of Jesus or just a wise man, he had enough light to see that one path was futile.

Today, humanity walks around in this darkness like it's normal. They can no longer see the light. Jesus preached and challenged the religious leaders of his day, telling them plainly that he was the light of the world. He punctuated his claim by performing miracles to prove his power and authority, but they were blind and could not see that the power he held translated to authority.

In their darkness, the Sanhedrin recognized some things that even the disciples didn't see initially. They saw his power and acknowledged it, but denied the source of that power. The religious leaders missed the important things about Jesus. They only saw him as a threat to their own authority.

What does it mean to walk in the light? If I have light, I can see where I am going and what I am doing. Light is also equated with knowledge.

The apostle Paul had a disciple named Demas, who was mentioned in three of Paul's letters. In Colossians 4:14 and Philemon 1:24, Demas sends his greetings to the churches. In 2 Timothy 4:10, it says that Demas forsook Paul because he loved the world more than Jesus. Demas had the knowledge of the light of the world, but didn't follow it.

Judas Iscariot not only abandoned Jesus, but he betrayed Jesus and turned him over to the Sanhedrin. The apostle Peter faltered, but repented of his actions and followed the light. Ananias and Sapphira lied to the Holy Spirit about their offering. They no doubt had heard Peter and the apostles preach the gospel. They were shown the light of the world, but pursued their own greed and the approval of man rather than God (Acts 5).

Jesus' light guides us in a path of righteousness. His light illuminates the hazards and stumbling blocks designed to trip us up. It points out temptations for what they are. It keeps us focused on the road leading to our Heavenly Father and not the lure of the darkness. As long as Peter kept his eyes on Jesus, he was able to walk on water. He took his eyes off the light of the world and slipped into the deep, dark waters.

Mankind had a dark and abysmal future until Jesus entered the world and gave us a hope and a future to look forward to. Jesus guides us away from sin and he is the light that guides us when we face decisions in our lives or dark times not pertaining to sin. When we face financial issues, choosing between jobs, how to handle difficult decisions, and so many more things. He is the reason I write. His light fuels my actions and my desires. When we see, understand, and follow him as the light of the world, our hearts are compelled to worship him. He is the light of the world and I'm a solar panel soaking it in. :)

SONG: *Here I Am to Worship* by various artists

PRAYER: Jesus, thank you for all that you went through to be a light for us.

Entertain

Finally, brothers and sisters, whatever is true, whatever is noble, whatever is right, whatever is pure, whatever is lovely, whatever is admirable—if anything is excellent or praiseworthy—think about such things. Whatever you have learned or received or heard from me, or seen in me—put it into practice. And the God of peace will be with you.
Philippians 4:8-9

PEOPLE WATCH MOVIES, television, play games, and read books for entertainment. It is an escape from reality. Sometimes we need those little getaways. The problems come in when we try to live in a fantasy world and never face the real world.

Here's one for all the Fantasy and Sci-Fi fans out there. We live in two dimensions at once. We live in God's kingdom as well as a physical principality. There are angels and demons around us that we do not see. To the Christian, the unseen doesn't always mean imaginary.

The Bible doesn't really deal with entertainment as a topic. In the Old Testament, when God taught the children of Israel about the law and what sacrifices to offer under what circumstances. He also set aside times of celebration. He had us set aside one day a week to rest and even the fields were given a period of rest every seven years.

Entertainment challenges the imagination. It gets us outside our comfortable boxes. Jesus asked questions that challenged the imagination such as asking two blind men, what do you want me to do for you? What could a man afflicted with blindness want that Jesus could offer? Do you suppose hours or days later, as the excitement wore off, they pondered that question a little further? Jesus also asked questions about why those around him feared or doubted. Do we have doubts and fears because we don't fully consider who God is and what he is capable of? We need to think beyond our own physical limitations step into, "What if..."

Speculative fiction answers a "what if" question. It challenges our understanding of events and their outcomes. It's good to be stretched and explore options. The apostle Paul tells us to spend time on the things that are good, admirable, pure, true, praiseworthy, and noble. Does that mean we need to limit ourselves to the Hallmark Channel? If that were true, there are things in the Bible we shouldn't read. What does the apostle Paul mean, then?

Jesus was pure and without sin. What he did was admirable, noble, and praiseworthy when he left heaven to come to Earth, live as one of us, and die for sins he never committed. Are there other stories that are noble and admirable? Is it true that Christians face death, pain, or suffering?

There are people who enjoy horror. I personally am not a big horror fan. I did enjoy watching a TV series known as *Criminal Minds*. After a steady diet of the show, I began to experience a dark heaviness in my spirit. Is it a sin to watch such things? Not unless it is one of those things that God specifically puts his finger on and tells you to abstain from it. Keeping a steady diet of dark entertainment can damage the spirit. There are some very dark circumstances mentioned in scripture, but the Bible doesn't dwell on those situations alone. There are stories of defeats and victories.

When we write stories, poems, novels, or screenplays, we can put them forth as entertainment—an escape from reality and an experiment in stretching the imagination. When Jesus walked on the water, he could have passed by without the disciples seeing him, or he could have simply vanished from one spot and reappeared on the opposite shore. He could have ridden the wind instead of walking. Why allow the disciples to see him walking on the water?

We often face difficult circumstances that we have no idea how we're going to get out of those situations. How many times has God surprised us with the way he rescues us? Our faith is strengthened when we remember that the God we serve is the God who can save his children from a fiery furnace, a den of lions, or walk them out the front door of a prison. He is a fire falling from Heaven, water walking, raise the dead to life God. I don't know about you, but I hope God took videos over the centuries and plans to show us some home movies when we get to Heaven someday. There are events mentioned in the Bible that I would love to see.

What we write displays our faith in God. It opens doors and possibilities. Having a Christian worldview affects the way we see things. Looking at an impossible situation, we can imagine and expect a miracle. In the scripture in Philippians listed above, Paul encourages us to reflect and contemplate the possibilities. In Matthew 7, Jesus tells us to ask, seek, and knock. He asked the blind man what he wanted. The blind man could have said he wanted riches, so he wouldn't have to beg anymore, or he could have asked Jesus to forgive his sins. Jesus tells us that if we ask, we will receive. If we seek him we will find. If we knock, the door will open. He doesn't say what we will receive, find, or which door will open, but knowing the God we serve, it will be worthwhile.

This is why we write with the goal of entertaining, because it opens wide the door of expectation, imagination, and hope. Through entertainment, the gospel may reach the hearts and minds of the reader in ways that nothing else will. God is a God of creativity. We are limited only by our imagination so let your imagination run wild.

SONGS: *Famous For (I Believe)* by Tauren Wells and *Steal My Show* by Toby Mac

PRAYER: Father, thank you for the gift of writing and may we use it to expand the faith of those who read what we write.

Shine Your Light

"You are the light of the world. A town built on a hill cannot be hidden. Neither do people light a lamp and put it under a bowl. Instead they put it on its stand, and it gives light to everyone in the house. In the same way, let your light shine before others, that they may see your good deeds and glorify your Father in heaven.

Matt 5:14-16

THIS PASSAGE IS FROM the Sermon on the Mount. Jesus has just gone through the Beatitudes and he's addressing a multitude of people from all walks of life. He is addressing the poor in spirit, the mourning, the meek, the spiritually hungry, the merciful, the pure, the peacemakers, and the persecuted. He knows where they are coming from and assures them that they are blessed—not that they will be blessed—but they are blessed right now.

These people have heard rumors about Jesus and are beginning to see miraculous events happening. They don't yet know who he really is. They've been looking for the Messiah to be a religious and military leader to free them from the Romans. Jesus turns the tables on them much like he overturned the tables in the temple.

God never intended for the children of Israel to be the only ones to see salvation. In Genesis 12:2-3, God promises Abram that he will make a great nation of his descendants, He will bless Abram, and Abram will be a blessing. The final line in verse 3 says, "in you all the families of the earth shall be blessed." The children of Israel weren't meant to keep God for themselves.

Isaiah 19:19-21 says,

"In that day there will be an altar to the Lord in the heart of Egypt, and a monument to the Lord at its border. It will be a sign and witness to the Lord Almighty in the land of Egypt. When they cry out to the Lord because of their oppressors, he will send them a savior and defender, and he will rescue them. So the Lord will make himself known to the Egyptians, and in that day they will acknowledge the Lord. They will worship with sacrifices and grain offerings; they will make vows to the Lord and keep them."

THE EGYPTIANS HAD SEEN God at work when he delivered the children of Israel from slavery. Even though it was many generations later, they had heard the stories and knew who God was.

In Isaiah 49:6b, the Lord says, "I will also make you a light for the Gentiles, that my salvation may reach to the ends of the earth." God never intended to limit his favor and forgiveness to the nation of Israel. Instead, his plan was to use his chosen people to be the vessel to convey his forgiveness and his blessing to the rest of the world.

In the Sermon on the Mount, Jesus tells the children of Israel that they are of the light of the world and you can't hide a city built up high. The Israelites were a city on display. God had blessed them through the ages and the surrounding nations could see it. In modern terms, it makes no sense to turn on a lamp then hide it where it can't be seen. Today we install lights in the ceiling so everyone who enters a room can see. A light is meant to be seen.

All children of God are a light to those around them. We are commanded to let our light to shine so others can see our good deeds and glorify our Heavenly Father. People don't need to look at us. They need to look at the results of our relationship with Jesus.

Many writers are introverts. If you are an introvert, it may be difficult to shine your light. Depending on exactly how introverted you are, it may seem nearly impossible for some. However, it's not impossible when we put things into perspective. We aren't trying to get others to look at us, but to see Jesus. People can be scary, but keep in mind God created every person who has ever lived on the Earth.

Talking to friends is easier than talking to strangers, and establishing common ground is a good way to make a new friend. God created every person you run into, so you do have something in common.

It's also easier to shine your light when you're excited about something. I am not very outgoing, but if I get excited about something, it's hard to silence me.

I've been a Christian for decades. If you ask me a question about the Bible, I'll gladly give you an answer or search out the answer if I can. Voluntarily sharing my personal walk with God is—personal. If our focus is in the wrong place, it can be uncomfortable. The light we have comes from him. It doesn't originate with us and it shouldn't stay with us. His light isn't meant to stay with us. It isn't supposed to be hidden.

Since sharing God with others is difficult for me, I've spent time searching and studying God's Word. I launched into prayers about sharing and witnessing. I prayed an honest, heartfelt prayer, asking God to task me with sharing him and expanding my introverted sphere of influence. God answered my prayer in so many ways.

If you are struggling with sharing from your introverted cocoon, God can provide for that need. It might be through what you write, sharing with one person, a post on social media, or an act of kindness. You have to start by getting your light out from under the bowl. Don't be afraid. Fear is the weapon of your enemy. God has entrusted you with his light. Shine for all the world to see.

SONGS: *Lights Shine Bright* by Toby Mac featuring Hollyn or *This Little Light of Mine* (children's song)

PRAYER: Jesus, show me how to shine your light for all to see.

Self-promotion vs Pride

I am talking to you Gentiles. Inasmuch as I am the apostle to the Gentiles, I take pride in my ministry in the hope that I may somehow arouse my own people to envy and save some of them. For if their rejection brought reconciliation to the world, what will their acceptance be but life from the dead? If the part of the dough offered as firstfruits is holy, then the whole batch is holy; if the root is holy, so are the branches.
Romans 11:13-16

WRITERS, ARTISTS, MUSICIANS, actors and others are told they have to market themselves along with their creation. The Bible is no stranger to humility and advising us to be humble. It denounces pride. Proverbs 16:18 says, "Pride goes before destruction, a haughty spirit before a fall." Yet in Psalms 47:4 the Israelites are called the "pride of Jacob."

We are proud when our children make the honor roll or avoid the mistakes we made in our younger days. We're proud of ourselves for Acing that test or making the Dean's List. So is pride a good thing or a bad one?

Pride is defined by Merriam-Webster's Dictionary in several ways. The first definition of pride is reasonable self-esteem, confidence in oneself, or self-respect. Now we cannot define right or wrong based on society because society has been wrong too many times. Having a certain amount of self-confidence or self-esteem doesn't sound unreasonable. If I were to paint a beautiful picture that came out perfectly, then said, "Oh, it's okay, but I should have done better," that lacks honesty.

The second definition of pride is pleasure from a relationship, association, achievement, or possession. I have always been proud of my husband as being the man who initiated the Wreaths Across America activities in the Chattanooga National Cemetery. We can feel pride at that item that was handed down to us from four generations ago. We can be proud of our membership in an organization like the Civil Air Patrol.

Paul took pride in his ministry, which means he didn't do it half-heartedly. His ministry reflected his zeal for Jesus. It's acceptable to take pride in your work and to be happy when you did a good job. The problem comes when it is carried too far.

The third definition of pride is exaggerated self-esteem or conceit. As false humility lacks honesty, so does conceit. The pride that reflects conceit says that we are above others, when we aren't.

Imagine standing at a table to sell your books and the person asks if your books are any good. What are you going to say to them? Pause to reflect on that question for a moment if you need to.

Personally, I write the types of things that I enjoy reading, but if you don't enjoy my particular genres, you might not enjoy them. Be honest when you self-promote and have self-confidence. Don't hyper-inflate yourself or your creation. If you look at your writing and say, "I did this all myself," then you aren't being honest. God gave you your love for writing, the mind of a creator, the education to write, the computer that you work on and the support staff to publish. God deserves praise and credit, too.

King Nebuchadnezzar became full of pride and looked at his kingdom as all his own doing. God took him down several notches by taking his kingdom and his mind from him. Pride is one of those middle of the road things. A little is necessary and good for you. A lot of pride is a sin.

What can you say when you self-promote? If you know you didn't do a good job with your work of art, perhaps you shouldn't be promoting it. If it's worth reading, you probably feel excited about it and it's easy to share your excitement. People will see the love you have for your work when your face lights up to share something about your book. That light can be a big selling point. You can tell them you have all five-star reviews or that your book won an award and those are honest selling points. If you don't have those options, expressing the comments of others who have read it takes your own opinion out of the equation. Ask yourselves these questions: 1) Did you do a good job with your writing? Including listening to the wisdom of your editor? 2) Would you recommend this book to someone to read even if you hadn't written it? 3) Is it a book you would read? If you answered yes to those questions, then tell others that. Tell them it's good or even great, if they like ____ genre. Don't try pushing a Fantasy book off on someone who is looking for Sci-Fi. Be honest and realize that even as you self-promote, your book isn't a fit for everyone.

Take pride in your work, but don't be consumed with pride. God gave you this gift. Offer it back to him as a gift of praise without being haughty or ashamed. Find the line down the middle of the road. Don't be afraid to share God's gift to you. You are his child and make your Father proud of you.

SONG: *Gold* by Britt Nicole

PRAYER: Father, guide my words and the attitude of my heart to have the zeal for the ministry without the trappings of conceit.

Parables are Stories

My people, hear my teaching; listen to the words of my mouth. I will open my mouth with a parable; I will utter hidden things, things from of old—things we have heard and known, things our ancestors have told us. We will not hide them from their descendants; we will tell the next generation the praiseworthy deeds of the Lord, his power, and the wonders he has done.
Psalm 78:1-4 A maskil of Asaph.

PARABLES ARE STORIES used to achieve an understanding of a particular point. As a parent, I have used stories to explain things to my children when they didn't understand something. A pastor uses verbal anecdotes, stories, or other illustrations to drive home a particular point. Jesus used parables as teaching points and to express his own understanding of the intentions of the Pharisees without making outright accusations.

According to Matthew Henry's commentary, Asaph, David's scribe, wrote the psalm above addressing the people under David's rule to strengthen them and remind them of the wonders God had performed for them. The Psalm is a historical account of the establishment of the law and his covenant with Israel. It related the miracles God performed for their ancestors in Egypt and the Israelites' rebellious nature, including the consequences of their disobedience.

Parables, or stories, can help us understand and remember important life lessons. There are numerous civilizations that didn't develop written language, so they used verbal stories to remember their history. My father was an elementary school history teacher, and much to his dismay, I never enjoyed studying history. I did enjoy learning about history from library books that told stories of historical figures starting from their childhood. Granted, they were probably considered historical *fiction*, but they were fairly accurate from a historical perspective. I daresay I learned more history from those stories than I ever learned in a classroom.

Stories aren't just for children. Jesus spoke to the adult population using stories or parables. Gideon speakers base their entire presentations on stories of lives that were changed by the placement of a Gideon Bible.

Were the parables about actual events or were they fictitious examples? Some people believe it was one and some believe the other. If it mattered, Jesus wouldn't have said, "a man," "a woman," "a landowner," or "a farmer." He would have called them by name. It wasn't the identity of the individual that was important, but the knowledge and understanding to be gleaned that was important.

As writers, when we present a message, sometimes the realness of an event is important. If I were to write a book dealing with overcoming some trauma, it might be best to present it from the perspective of a victim who has dealt with that trauma. Writing a story to illustrate God's love or mercy would probably have a stronger impact coming from a true story, but often people use fiction to escape reality. They might want something darker than their own circumstances to make whatever they are facing seem less painful. A cozy mystery might give the brain a good exercise in critical thinking. Romantic comedies could lift the spirit. Action adventure dramas can get the blood circulating.

Many would argue that all you need is the Bible. That is true. Yet, how many people refuse to pick up a Bible because it's old, or boring, or whatever? If I can get someone intrigued by a Fantasy, Sci-Fi,

Dystopian, Steampunk, or some other genre of story showing God's grace and mercy, then perhaps they may become curious enough to pick up a Bible.

Like a hammer, a parable is a tool which can be used for good or for evil. A hammer can be used to build a house or destroy a house. A parable can be used the same way. Jesus didn't use his parables for evil, but he did use the parable of the vineyard and the tenants to reveal the evil in the hearts of the Pharisees (Matthew 21:33-46).

One of the most powerful parables was the one about the prodigal son (Luke 15:11-32) because it shows the depth of God's love for his children. Again, no names were mentioned, but it is the demonstration of God's love and forgiveness that matters. There are so many powerful truths in that parable. It speaks of his lost children coming home; the Father running to us when we return, greeting us with love and compassion, clothing us in a robe of righteousness, and preparing a place for us at his table.

I have two songs for you this time. Both have been around since the mid-80's but they are both about the Prodigal Son. I hope you enjoy both of them.

SONGS: *The Prodigal Son Suite* by Keith Green, and *When God Ran* by Benny Hester

PRAYER: Father, help me share all the wondrous things that you have done both in my life and in the days of old.

Plans

"For I know the plans I have for you," declares the Lord, "plans to prosper you and not to harm you, plans to give you hope and a future."
Jeremiah 29:11

"For my thoughts are not your thoughts, neither are your ways my ways," declares the Lord. "For as the heavens are higher than the earth, So are My ways higher than your ways, And My thoughts than your thoughts."
Isaiah 55:8

THE THINGS WE NEED to see based on the scriptures above are:

1. God has a plan for us.
2. Commit what we do to the Lord.
3. Realize that his plans may look and seem crazy, but God isn't limited like we are.

THE BIBLE HAS SEVERAL things to say about plans. God has plans on top of plans laid down for all of us since the beginning of time. When God said, "Let there be light" and began his creation of the universe, he knew what sins we would commit and the immense pain and suffering that his beloved son would have to go through to redeem humanity. He also knew that not everyone would accept his son's sacrifice. Even though he created every single human, he knew many of those who are and were precious to him would remain lost—but God put his plans in place for all of creation.

From where we sit today and the horrible things that are happening in the world, we often have to wonder why God would care enough to have anything to do with this world anymore. He wiped out the world once with a flood, saving the only righteous man on the planet. The children of Israel went through vicious cycles of righteousness and rebellion. God put plans into place to discipline them and bring them back to him. They would return, grow complacent, fall into worshiping idols again, and the cycle would repeat. Despite their sin, God never wiped out his people completely. Many did die, but there was always hope for the future, as mentioned in Jeremiah 29:11.

As God had a plan for humanity as a whole, he has plans for each individual. He knows where we started, what we've been through, and the most important thing he knows is what is ahead of us. He's already seen the next hour, week, year, and our final day. Who's better qualified to make plans for us? That doesn't mean we don't make plans at all. It means we plan with his plans in mind.

There are times when we plan our day, but nothing goes the way we planned. How do we handle it when our plans fall apart? Did our plans crumble because we planned wrongly? Did we miss something? Did we do something wrong? Or is it possible that things went exactly the way God intended? Have you ever had one of those mornings when you have a long list of things to do and suddenly your car keys are missing or your tire is flat? We've all had days like that. It's frustrating. I've looked for those lost keys in the places where they should have been, only to find them in the place I had already looked.

Why do these things happen? Is it because there's too much on our minds and we aren't focused on where we're looking? Maybe, or is it because God had a different plan for our day? His plans are so far removed from us, some things we may never understand. Because our day didn't start as early as we wanted, did we avoid a traffic accident? Was there someone out there who needed us to minister to them by just saying "hi," or smiling at them and we might have missed the opportunity if we were on *our* timetable?

What do you do when your day and your plans go awry? Do you pitch a fit? Cry? Get angry? Do you make life miserable for the people you run into? Do you consider that every day is a gift from God and it's our job to use that day in a way that brings glory to him? God knew how your day was going to start. He saw this day coming before you were even born. No day has ever dawned that he didn't have planned. Let me say that again. Whether it's the best day, worst day, or the dullest day in your life, God knows about it and he is ready for it.

What if it's more than one day's plans that don't work like we want it to? It's important to set goals for our lives and plans to support our goals.

When I graduated from high school, I wanted to write and direct Christian plays and musicals. My plan was to study theology to be certain that what I wrote was Biblically sound. I made plans, changed plans, and didn't hit anything right off the bat. I spent the next twenty-five years doing everything but writing. My plans were not God's plans. When our children started growing up and leaving home, I prayed a frantic, fearful prayer about what to do with my life once the nest was empty. I committed my future to his plan. His plan has been so far above my plans. God gave me twenty-five years of learning and life experiences, then brought me back to my plans to write. God's plan has my cup full, pressed down, shaken together, and running over.

Whether it is one day's plans or our lifetime plans, we may not always know what his plans are accomplishing, but if we follow his heart and his direction, we will accomplish what he wants for us. How do we know what his plans are for us? We do that by listening to him, studying his Word, and acting on things that we know to be his will, even if it might seem a little strange to us. Joshua had to send his troops to march in circles around Jericho. Joseph's life didn't go like he planned either. Do you think as a young man raised and educated in the affluent household of Pharaoh, Moses expected to become a fugitive and to challenge Pharaoh's power? Ezekiel was sent to preach to a valley of dry bones. Ask Jonah what happens when we don't follow God's plans for us.

His plans are bigger and better than our plans. He knows us better than we know ourselves. Do you have what it takes to follow his plans? God's plans aren't for cowards, but the rewards are beyond belief.

SONG: *God of All My Days* by Casting Crowns

PRAYER: Father, help me to trust you and commit to your plans.

Using God's Gifts

Each of you should use whatever gift you have received to serve others, as faithful stewards of God's grace in its various forms. If anyone speaks, they should do so as one who speaks the very words of God. If anyone serves, they should do so with the strength God provides, so that in all things God may be praised through Jesus Christ. To him be the glory and the power for ever and ever. Amen.

1 Peter 4:10-11

"USE IT OR LOSE IT," is a popular phrase in several circles. If you decided to stop using your right hand and make your left hand do everything, your right hand would lose its dexterity. A runner who is accustomed to running several miles per week has to keep up their pace or they'll become unable to run the same distances.

Each of us are given gifts and talents. God gave them to us for a reason. Sometimes we may struggle to know what our gifts and talents are, but once we identify them, God expects us to use those gifts for his glory. In the parable of the talents (aka bags of gold), the man who hid his money and didn't put it to good use had it taken from him.

The gifts God gave to each of us aren't strictly for our own use. The apostle Peter, in the scripture above, says to use your gifts to serve others. If we have the gift of baking the best apple pies ever, but we never share that gift, we are not being good stewards of God's gift to us.

In this section of Peter's letter, he admonishes the reader first to pray and be in a mindset to pray. The second thing he says is to love each other deeply, not love self deeply. There is a line between caring for self and caring only for self. We are to be hospitable and not whine and complain about it and use our gifts to serve others. It doesn't mean we can't use them for self, but we aren't using them only for ourselves. If you speak, do so as though you are speaking the words of God. Your words should not be hateful or disparaging. Serving others can be difficult and draining. God provides the strength and the grace, needed to serve others.

When I published my first book, my sales were abysmal. They aren't great even now, but that isn't the point. My husband and I put a lot of work and a significant amount of money into the book, and it didn't make a profit. Naturally, I was tempted to give up. Through prayer, God showed me that success isn't always measured in monetary profits. God showed me where my successes were. My life had changed and writing had been an answer to prayer. There were people who were enjoying my books and hounding me for the next one. God changed my life by giving me the gift of writing. If I kept that gift to myself and didn't share it with others, I would rob God of his glory, myself of joy, and my fans of the pleasure of reading my books.

God gives his children such a variety of gifts. We may not use every gift all the time. When teaching, sometimes a teacher must take a sabbatical to rest and learn for a time before returning to teaching.

Do you have a gift that you've hidden away that you've failed to use in a while? Are you afraid to use that gift because you don't think you are that good or you might fail? Perhaps it is time to re-evaluate. Get that dusty gift out of the back of your closet, polish it up, and use it to bring glory to God. Don't keep it buried like the one servant did with his bag of gold. God can bring that gift back to life.

SONG: *Rattle* by Elevation Worship

PRAYER: Jesus, show us how to love and serve others using the gifts you have given us.

You Are Not Alone

What you're doing is not good, Moses' father-in-law said to him. You will certainly wear out both yourself and these people who are with you, because the task is too heavy for you. You can't do it alone. Now listen to me; I will give you some advice, and God be with you. You be the one to represent the people before God and bring their cases to him. Instruct them about the statutes and laws, and teach them the way to live and what they must do. But you should select from all the people able men, God-fearing, trustworthy, and hating bribes. Place them over the people as commanders of thousands, hundreds, fifties, and tens.
Exodus 18:17-21

WRITING A NOVEL CAN be a daunting task. Novels start around 50,000 words and go up from there. If you self-publish, you are responsible for your cover, editing, proofing, formatting, publishing, and marketing. There are also the copyright forms, library of congress application, and more. If you publish traditionally, you still need a literary agent and get a publisher to pick up your manuscript. These days, marketing falls more heavily on the author than the publisher.

The act of writing by itself requires a lot of work. Characters have to be created, worlds are built, and a conflict established whether you are writing a flash fiction, an epic novel, or anything in between. If you're writing non-fiction, there are similar areas of development. Research is involved in both areas of writing. Then, you, as the writer, write all the words. You shed blood, sweat, and tears over what to say and how to say it.

In Genesis, God gave Adam the creative task of naming all the animals. God decided it wasn't good for Adam to be alone and none of the animals were quite the companion he needed. God created Eve to be a helpmate for Adam.

Moses' father-in-law, Jethro, saw Moses trying to tackle the unbelievable task of shepherding the disorganized, disbelieving, rebellious children of Israel and settling every petty dispute among them. Jethro wisely advised Moses to share his load with the resources God provided for him.

God trains some to be writers, illustrators, publishers, marketers, editors of varying specialties, and some to be techies. You don't have to be all things. It should always be our goal to learn to do more and to do what we do better, but we don't have to do it all. God expects us to use the resources he gives to us. God gave Moses a wise father-in-law and leaders that he could depend on and delegate to.

It's easy for us to want to maintain control. As the saying goes, "If you want something done right, do it yourself." That isn't always best.

Personally, I have a decent handle on spelling and grammar, but I miss things. Yes, I proof and edit my writing, but then I hand it to someone else because it's easy to overlook things.

It's never good to give in to stubbornness and refuse to allow others to help you. If Moses had kept going the way he was, what could have happened? Burnout, resentment, and exhaustion are just three possibilities. Joshua may have been called upon to take over leading Israel earlier. He spent forty years learning under Moses and being prepared for his role of leader. What if he had inherited Moses' habit of doing it all himself?

When I started writing, I was scared to death. It was an answer to prayer, but I had never seriously spoken to my husband about it in the first twenty years of our marriage. I wasn't sure how my husband was going to receive the idea.

I like to think I have always been the helpmate God called me to be to my husband. I made some mistakes, but overall I have supported him. Now that I was embarking on this new journey, I wondered how my husband was going to feel about it. God was already providing for me on this journey. My husband was glad and excited to join me in this endeavor. It seems that all we've done together, whether it was at my husband's leading or mine, we've worked well together. God knew what we needed and provided for each of us. At every turn, whatever resources we've needed, God has provided.

As writers, when we have questions about anything, we have groups on social media to consult. There are classes to take, software to use, experts to hire, critique groups, and more. God knows what we need and provides for our needs if we have the wisdom to use it. Sometimes we have to take our hands off of a thing and give it over to another. Whatever we write is dear to us and we want it to be the way we want it. We also want it to be accepted by industry standards.

Moses listened to Jethro. He didn't try to hang onto the control. He delegated the things he could. Moses followed God and represented God to the people and trained his people accordingly.

Unless you hire a ghostwriter, you have to be the one to write your story. Certain things you can't pass off, nor should you, but don't be afraid to let someone else handle the things you don't have to. Use the resources God gave you. Don't wear yourself out. It's not good for you to be alone or do it all alone.

SONG: *Let Go, Let God* by Jack Cassidy

PRAYER: Father, give us the resources we need and the wisdom to use them to bring glory to your name through the writing you gave us to do.

Bearing One Another's Burdens

Therefore, encourage one another and build each other up, just as in fact you are doing.
1 Thessalonians 5:11

WE ARE ALL UNIQUE. Several of us may have similar qualities, but no two people are exactly alike. I have strengths and weaknesses, as do you. My strengths or weaknesses are not necessarily yours. As writers, some are plotters and others are not. Some can write fantasy or romance—others couldn't pull it off, no matter how hard they try. You may be a seasoned writer or struggling to finish your first written work. What we have in common is: we are writers seeking to honor God with writing.

Writing comes easily to some and to others it's a struggle. One way we can honor God with our writing is to react differently than the world reacts and view other writers as competition. I Corinthians 3:9 says, "For we are co-workers in God's service; you are God's field, God's building."

It is easy to criticize others and find fault with them or their work. The apostle Paul tells the Thessalonians to encourage one another and build each other up. Does that mean you tell someone their work is great when it clearly isn't? No—there are kind ways to lead and instruct someone in how to make their craft better.

There have been many times I look at what I've written and doubted myself or what I've written. When I attended one of my first writer's conferences, I came away discouraged because I saw all the things I was doing wrong. A friend, who is not a writer, gave me a simple word of encouragement. He said, "You have a good story." Those words changed my life. I knew I had made mistakes in how I published my books, but they were fixable mistakes and that I shouldn't give up.

A few years later, I reached a point where I taught a class about how to write and publish books. I'm no expert, but I've learned a few things and wanted to share them with those who were just getting started. In the class, we discussed what the definition of a successful writer was. The definitions were anywhere from somebody who gets something on paper to someone who earns their living off writing. I don't earn a living from writing, but I have fans, and I sell a few books. I still consider myself a successful writer because lives are being changed by what I do. Sometimes my life is the one being changed and sometimes, it's someone else's life.

I attended a writers' retreat where each writer was in a different place. Some were struggling with their plot, others were just getting started, some needed motivation to begin again, and others just needed to be away from everyday distractions. I watched through the three-day retreat as the participants helped each other work through problems and the words flowed.

Words are powerful. They can build you up or tear you down. What you write and what you say can be a source of encouragement to another writer. Don't be afraid to seek help from your peers to improve your work. Encourage each other and build each other up.

SONG: *Speak Life* by Toby Mac

PRAYER: Let the words of my mouth, and the meditation of my heart, be acceptable in thy sight, O Lord, my strength, and my redeemer. Psalm 19:14 (KJV)

Impostor Syndrome

The Lord turned to him and said, "Go in the strength you have and save Israel out of Midian's hand. Am I not sending you?"
"Pardon me, my lord," Gideon replied, "but how can I save Israel? My clan is the weakest in Manasseh, and I am the least in my family."
Judges 6:14-15
Recommended reading Judges 6:12-18

IMPOSTOR SYNDROME IS the belief that you don't deserve a particular title, or that you aren't worthy of your success, or even the success that others attribute to you. Impostor syndrome is a cousin to doubt. Most writers will suffer from impostor syndrome at some point in their careers and the reasons may vary.

First, let's look at what some of the definitions of a writer are. A writer can be someone who writes, or someone who writes and is published. Of course, the doubts start right here. "Well, I've been writing but I've not finished anything," or "I'm not published yet." At this point in time, you could call yourself a writer or not. That part is your own decision.

What about the definition of a successful writer? Is it someone who has published a book? Does being self-published count? Are you a success if, as being self-published, you make enough to pay for the costs of editing and book covers? Do you have to be making a living writing to be a successful writer?

In Judges 6, Gideon is threshing wheat. He's farming. An angel comes along and greets him, calling him a mighty warrior and telling him the Lord was with him (v. 12). The Hebrew word for "you" is singular, not plural. The angel is referring to Gideon, not the nation of Israel. Gideon turns it around and inquires about the Lord being "with us," not him (v. 13). He's pushing the things he doesn't want to hear away.

God tasks Gideon with defending Israel against the Midianites. Gideon immediately gives the Angel several reasons why this can't happen. Gideon recognizes that he's just a farmer, hiding his crop in a wine press to keep the Midianites from finding it. He's the least in his family (probably meaning the youngest), his entire clan is the weakest in the tribe of Manasseh, and Manasseh is one of the smallest tribes of Israel. One couldn't get much lower in rank as far as Gideon was concerned. Gideon remembered the tales of God bringing the people out of Egypt and the wonders performed along the way, but somehow he forgot that in his family history, the younger was often blessed and used by God ahead of the older ones. Isaac blessed Esau, but said he would serve his younger brother. When Jacob blessed Joseph's sons, he proclaimed that the tribe of Ephraim would be greater than his brother Manasseh. Joseph himself was one of the youngest of Jacob's sons, and God used Joseph to save all of Israel, Egypt, and people from many other nations.

Gideon had no reason to believe he deserved to be used by God, to be a mighty warrior, or a savior of the nation of Israel. He goes on to request several signs as proof that this is what God wanted from him. If anybody had impostor syndrome, it had to be Gideon—but he wasn't the only one.

Jonah quite probably suffered from impostor syndrome. He goes to Nineveh and prophecies of its destruction but the people repent and the city is spared. Was Jonah mistaken? No, but I suspect he felt foolish because he said God told him the city was going to be destroyed and it wasn't.

Moses was another one who faced such a struggle. He was an escaped criminal from Egypt. He was raised in Pharaoh's household, well-educated, but he was not an Egyptian. He was a shepherd which Egyptians looked down on, and an escaped Hebrew slave. Talk about being at the bottom of the societal ladder. He also had a speech impediment. God calls him to free all the Hebrew slaves in Egypt by facing down Pharaoh, who knew Moses had rejected his upbringing and killed an Egyptian. Moses didn't feel comfortable or worthy of the task God gave him.

Was Gideon a mighty warrior? Was Moses a liberator and a great leader?Gideon and Moses did not view themselves in those roles, but those who followed them did.

There are a lot of reasons why someone might feel like they don't deserve the title of writer or author. In addition to the ones mentioned earlier, there are some others such as not being properly trained as a writer. Perhaps you don't have a degree in English, Literature, or Journalism. Not knowing the finer points of writing isn't what makes or breaks the definition of a writer. It's better to learn as much as you can about points of view, character development, and story arcs, but knowing those don't make you a writer. You aren't a fraud just because you don't know all the technical points of writing. You can't trick people into liking your stories. Writing makes you a writer.

I struggled with impostor syndrome too. My book sales don't break the bank and I've never won an award for any of my books or stories. Do you know what makes me a writer? I write. I have people that are anxious to get my next books (aka fans) and people that love the stories I've told. I was a writer long before I published my first story. When I struggled, wondering if anyone would even like them, I decided that if no one but me was touched by what I wrote; it was enough. More lives have been touched since publishing than my own. God tasked me with this and I find fulfillment in this task.

I have a prayer that I am praying for you, the reader and writer based on 2 Thessalonians 1:11, "With this in mind, we constantly pray for you, that our God may make you worthy of his calling, and that by his power he may bring to fruition your every desire for goodness and your every deed prompted by faith."

PRAYER: Father, I pray that the writers who are reading this devotional be worthy of your calling, and by your power bring to fruition their desire for goodness and their writing be prompted by faith.

SONG: *Nobody* by Casting Crowns & Matthew West

Loneliness

The Lord God said, "It is not good for the man to be alone. I will make a helper suitable for him."
Genesis 2:18

SOME PEOPLE ARE EXTROVERTS who thrive on socialization and others are introverts who crave solitude. We all overlap the boundaries between introvert and extrovert—there is no ultimate introvert or extrovert. I did the Myers-Briggs personality test and determined that I am 53% introvert and 47% extrovert.

At one point in time in my life, I would have considered myself an extrovert. In college, I loved getting out with my friends and having fun. The reason I became a writer is that I was afraid of being alone at home. My kids were growing up and leaving home and I got scared. God gave me the task of writing because it isn't good for man (anyone) to be alone—and no, I don't think the characters in my head are real.

Writing has changed who I am. I enjoy getting out and socializing, but I also want those times alone with my thoughts and my characters. The problem of loneliness occurs when we don't have a balance between solitude and socialization. In my day job, I am a nurse. Nurses aren't big writers. I often feel isolated because my friends at work don't relate to what is now a major part of my life.

When Covid hit and the country shut down, my introverted writer friends were pretty happy and content. The extroverts suffered terribly from the isolation during that time. By the time the shut downs were over, even the most introverted people became lonely and needed to socialize.

Loneliness can happen when you feel there is no one around that relates to you, has anything in common with you, cares about you, or has time to spend with you. Genesis 2:18 talks about Adam in the garden of Eden. Can you imagine if God hadn't created Eve, how lonely Adam would have been? Could the lion understand Adam's tiredness at the end of a hard day working in the garden? Would a koala share the same joy of walking with God through the garden in the cool of the day?

Loneliness can also result from fear. Fear of people or their opinions of you can cause you to shut people out of your life. Fear that you'll do or say something socially unacceptable can cause you to distance yourself from others.

God doesn't want us to be alone. He wants us to have people in our lives that we can relate to, have some commonality with, and have time to spend with us. Writers are unique in what they do and in how they do it. It often requires solitude to gather your thoughts and organize them into a cohesive story. There's nothing wrong with being alone and a lot of things right with being alone. Jesus had to go to secluded places in the early hours of the morning to be alone and pray.

There is a time to be alone, but balance is important. Not making time for relationships creates isolation and loneliness. If you find yourself suffering from loneliness, perhaps it is time to establish a support system to counteract your loneliness. Have lunch regularly with a friend. Find a prayer partner. Join a writer's support group or if you have enough extrovert in you, start one. It is important to set aside time with like-minded people. There are times when the isolation hits me and I get on a video chat with a writer friend. Going to a writers' conference or retreat is also a great way to establish relationships with people who care and understand what a plot hole or writers' block is.

You don't have to limit yourself to socializing with writers. We need to spend time with other writers, but sometimes that isn't possible. You can also associate with people that you share other interests with such as golfers, gardeners, or any other area of interest. My coworkers don't share my interest in writing, but we can discuss cooking, child-rearing, healthcare, and several other topics. Being with someone, even if they aren't writers is better than being with no one.

Ecclesiastes 3 says there is a time and a season for everything. Too much solitude can lead to loneliness. We need time to be alone and time to be with others. Too much of either is detrimental to our own well-being. Jesus had times when he was thronged by crowds, times when he was with his core group, and times when he was alone with the Father.

There is a difference between being alone and being lonely. One can be lonely in a crowd. Cultivate those personal friendships. If you don't have a friend, then be a friend to someone else in need. Find that stranger who enters your church service, or that person who always comes by themselves. You don't have to be a people magnet or the popular person. Sometimes the popular people that everyone flocks around are the loneliest people.

If fear of people is the problem, God can intervene. Pray for release from fear and loneliness. Psalm 68:6 says, "God sets the lonely in families..." For those prone to loneliness God provides for them. A family, whether it is the one we are born into or one we've adopted, is the group of people who love and support us. They are the people who accept us, in spite of our faults and quirks. The apostle Paul tells the church in Galatia to carry each other's burdens, and that includes the burdens of loneliness or fear.

SONG: *Oh, My Soul* by Casting Crowns

PRAYER: Heavenly Father, set us in the family you have prepared for us and give us the courage to be a part of the relationships you have for us.

Creation

So God created mankind in his own image, in the image of God he created them; male and female he created them.
Genesis 1:27

THERE'S BEEN A THEOLOGICAL debate about whether mankind can actually create. The argument is that only God can create. Ecclesiastes 1:9 says, "What has been will be again, what has been done will be done again; there is nothing new under the sun."

As writers, we see the same tropes appear over and over again. Sometimes roles will be reversed, and sometimes an ending catches us unaware, but it has likely been done somewhere. How many remakes of movies have you seen? It's hard to see anything that's fresh and unique.

Obviously, we are not God, and we cannot speak anything into existence. By that definition, no, we cannot create.

God created man in his own image. Did he make us as something that resembles him physically or spiritually? There's been a lot of speculation about that. The list of witnesses who have seen God is rather small, so speculation is about all that we have. He speaks of having a throne to sit on and the Earth as his footstool. Mark 16:19 says that Jesus was taken up into heaven to sit at God's right hand. A throne suggests a body capable of sitting. A footstool suggests the presence of feet and right hands generally also have left hands opposite them. Noah found favor in God's eyes. Incense was offered as a pleasing aroma to God in the temple. Are these terms used because it relates to us in a way we can understand or are they more literal? Does it matter if we get our looks from our Heavenly Father?

God is a creator. He created everything that exists. Why did he create? Because he enjoyed it, perhaps? Did he create us to bring glory and praise to him? If we are true followers of Christ, can we do otherwise?

Some people, when they cook, have to follow the recipe verbatim. Others don't use recipes and still others fall somewhere in between. If you've ever looked up a recipe online, you will find dozens of different recipes for the same dish, whether it's brownies or meatloaf. There is no one way to make it. You will also find a list of substitutions if you get into a recipe and discover you're missing an ingredient. I might use a recipe as a guide, but I'm not likely to make anything the same way twice. However I make it, my meatloaf is still meatloaf even if it isn't made the same way. Is this creating?

Many people have hobbies, or even jobs where they create, build, or design things. A child builds a castle in the sand, draws a picture on a paper, or makes some shape out of colored clay. An architect designs buildings and the more money one has, the more intricate the design. Some arrange flowers, sew quilts, carve wooden statues, or paint pictures. Are writing stories any different, and did we get this characteristic from our Heavenly Father? What was Adam's first job? To give names to all the animals. Was that creating?

When a child is born, the parents are excited and love to see the likenesses the child has with its parents. Later, when the child begins to mimic some of our attitudes, we are sometimes less enthused. This infant is a beautiful creation that only God can truly take credit for. Creation is all around us. Every day, God paints a new sunrise and a new sunset. Even if we gave birth to twenty children, each one would be a new creation from the same set of genes.

We don't have the power of creation that God has, but part of our legacy is the desire to create things of beauty. How many times did you make some drawing or art project and couldn't wait to give it to your parent? When you handed that project to them, what were you looking for? A trophy to put on a shelf? An award ribbon or certificate? You wanted the approval of your parent and to see a smile on their face.

God made every one of us unique. There are no two snowflakes just alike. If I tried to draw the same picture twice, it wouldn't come out exactly the same no matter how many times I tried. Even though there is nothing new under the sun, in Christ we become new creations. When Jesus saves us, we become a new creation, a new person is born. Our DNA hasn't changed, but something inside us has changed.

God saw his creation and declared it to be "good." The day we are born again, we inherit a love for our Heavenly Father and a desire to please him. Like the prodigal son, we know we aren't worthy to be called his child, but we still desire to be even a servant in the father's house. Our Heavenly Father rejoices over us when we return to him because we were lost and dying in our sin, but have returned to him.

Like our Heavenly Father, we desire to create something good. We get such genetic traits from the one who created us. No, we don't have the ability to create perfect creations or something from nothing, like God does. We create within the limits of our humanness, whether it is a piece of artwork, a humanitarian project, or some other venture. God gave us the creativity gene and what we create gives praise and glory back to him.

SONGS: *Heart of the Father* by Ryan Ellis and *God of Wonders* by Third Day

PRAYER: Father, you created my entire being. Create a pure heart in me, O God, and renew a steadfast spirit within me.

Writer's Block

I waited patiently for the Lord; he turned to me and heard my cry. He lifted me out of the slimy pit, out of the mud and mire; he set my feet on a rock and gave me a firm place to stand. He put a new song in my mouth, a hymn of praise to our God. Many will see and fear the Lord and put their trust in him.

Psalm 40:1-3

THE DREADED *Writer's Block.* Like the scripture above, it can be described as a slimy pit of mud and mire. Have you ever been stuck in mud? Or maybe your car's been stuck in the mud? There was one time, as a small child, I dropped my ball and it rolled into some mud. I left the sidewalk to retrieve it and my feet got stuck. If I had pulled any harder, I would have walked out of my shoes because that mud wasn't going to let go. My father came and lifted me out of the mud and retrieved my ball.

The first step in solving a problem is identifying the problem. Writer's block can happen for a number of reasons, the first possible reason being that our schedule is so crowded with important events that we have trouble justifying taking the time to write. We walk past that computer or notebook and our neglected projects cry out for attention. Then when you have that brief period where you can write, but your conscience stabs at you for all the other things you think you should be doing instead. Or you are so lost you don't remember the story or where it was going.

A second reason for being unable to write is going through physical, psychological, or emotional trauma. If your mind is consumed with life events, there may be little room left for creativity. Illness, relationship issues, financial worries, or even just changes such as moving, changing jobs, etc., can use up all your creative energy. Sometimes a change in medications can hinder your ability to think and focus.

A third reason for writer's block can happen when you have the time, the energy, and even the focus, but the words just refuse to come. These issues are usually related to not being sold on your own story. The plot is headed a direction you don't want it to go or something just doesn't feel right about it. Sometimes the threat of a looming deadline can hinder you.

Ecclesiastes 3 reminds us that there is a season for all things and this may not be the season for writing in your life. If you are going through a difficult time, it might be the time to journal about your circumstances and lay your project aside for a time.

The second step in solving a problem is to pray about the problem and seek God's guidance. Psalm 40:1 begins by saying, "I waited patiently for the Lord..." Pay attention to the word—*patiently*. We don't just wait. We are to be patient. When the time is right, he will lift us out of whatever has us stuck. When that happens, he will set our feet on solid ground. When we come out of that darker, seemingly unproductive time, we will have new, richer, fuller ideas. As the Psalm suggests, God will give us a new song of praise and it will be a beacon of light and hope for others.

While identifying your problem, including its cause, and praying for the solution, watch out for the self-fulfilling prophecy. Don't sit and worry that you may never be able to write again. The writing may have stopped for one reason and then fear and worry set in, adding more pressure until one day you give up. There isn't anything wrong with choosing to stop writing, but giving up is another problem. I can change careers, change my mind about what I want to eat, or what to wear. There's nothing wrong with choosing not to write, but quitting due to fear is giving in to the enemy. Luke 6:45 says, "A good man brings good things out of the good stored up in his heart, and an evil man brings evil things out of the evil stored up in his heart. For the mouth speaks what the heart is full of." Don't let your heart be full of defeat and talk yourself into failure. Proverbs 4:23 says, "Above all else, guard your heart, for everything you do flows from it."

Here are some practical things you can do to take the pressure off:

- Set aside the project you are stuck on and work on something new for a while.
- Cut yourself some slack for deciding to write and putting off mowing the lawn for a day or two.
- If you are writing to please God, your writing is an offering to God with a pleasing aroma (2 Corinthians 2:14-15). If you find yourself stuck, reread what you've written, and make changes where you think things are going wrong.
- Identify your situation, pray about it, and make a change either in what you're doing, how you're doing it, or why you're doing it.

Once you've done all these things, wait patiently for the Lord to lift you up and put you on solid ground.

SONG: *He Brought Me Out*, a hymn written by Henry J. Zelley in 1898

PRAYER: Father, hear our cry. Rescue us from the mud and mire we are stuck in and place us back on your firm ground.

Sorrows into Joy

You turned my wailing into dancing; you removed my sackcloth and clothed me with joy,
Psalm 30:11

WRITING A BOOK, A STORY, or a poem is a lot of work. Hours, days, weeks, months, and sometimes years go into crafting your masterpiece. You create worlds that don't exist, characters who are never born, and give them personalities, conflicts, and flaws. You research history, science, mathematics, and more when trying to make your story a believable fiction.

Once the work is complete, the edits come, and the proofreading, and more edits and more proofreading. Of course, we can't forget designing a cover and *my personal favorite*, writing the book blurb. (NOT!) Somewhere in there is the legal and business stuff like getting your ISBN and Copyright. For those who publish independently, this is all your responsibility. A traditional publisher eliminates some of those struggles for you, but finding an agent and a publisher to accept your story is another struggle.

The process of writing can bring great joy. The imagination gets to run wild and do what it does best. It can be a happy escape from real life struggles and, depending on the author, you could be glad you don't suffer what the characters do.

In the process of writing, it's easy to hit walls, stumbling blocks, and potholes. Life happens and writing has to be set aside for a time, leaving a burning desire unquenched. You write yourself into a corner and can't find a way out. The dreaded writer's block gets you. How many times have you wanted to quit, pull your hair out, or bang your head against a wall?

Life is a struggle and writing imaginary struggles doesn't make them affect us any less. I've written about tragic deaths, and the heartfelt pains of my characters that made me cry. I've also laughed at humorous situations in my books.

Through blood, sweat, and tears, we work until that day comes. One exciting day, your final product, the book, arrives in the mail. The cover is shiny, the smell of fresh paper and ink waft from its pages, and your name is on the cover. Your picture is on the back. All the anguish and sorrow have paid off. Holding that book in your hand brings amazing joy. It doesn't matter if you haven't sold any books yet, it's still a joy like no other. The fruit of your labor is in your hands.

If you are still in the heat of the battle, and haven't published that first book yet, hang in there. The fight and the sorrow are worth it to have the joy that comes later. Today may not be that day, but tomorrow hasn't arrived.

Jesus tells us in John 16:33 that we will have trouble but that he has overcome the world. I spent many years working, going to school, raising a family, and not writing. I don't regret those things, although I would have preferred remaining a stay-at-home mom. We've endured financial hardships, physical hardships, and some nasty bumps in the road.

When God answered my prayers and brought me to a place where I could write, my rough road brought me to a place of joy. I get excited about displaying God's love and care for me through both the fiction and the nonfiction that I write. Sometimes the question comes up, "Does God not do enough miracles in real life that we have to pretend?" God has worked genuine miracles in my life many times. I still enjoy the idea of being a hero in a foreign land, a different world, or in space, but I would not dream of going to those places without God.

The Lord is the source of creation and the source of my joy. He has clothed me with joy and removed my sackcloth. I have had many joys in real life, meeting and marrying my husband, giving birth to my children, getting my degree in nursing, and others. My husband and I have reached a point where we are living our greatest joy. We work together to write and publish. Being where God wants me is the happiest time in my life.

No matter how many books I publish, I'm still going to have that broad smile across my face and a surge of adrenaline when that package arrives with my brand new book that I worked so hard to put together. God put all the pieces into place to bring those moments about. I'm smiling even now as I write this devotional.

SONG: *Overcomer* by Mandisa

PRAYER: Jesus, thank you for carrying us through the struggles and sorrow to the point of joy.

A Time to Laugh & Dance

There is a time for everything, and a season for every activity under the heavens: a time to be born and a time to die, a time to plant and a time to uproot, a time to kill and a time to heal, a time to tear down and a time to build, a time to weep and a time to laugh, a time to mourn and a time to dance.
Ecclesiastes 3:1-4

EVERYONE FACES UPS and downs. We have good days and bad days. Times of darkness or depression can seem to last an eternity, and joyous times are over way too soon. Ecclesiastes three tells us to expect the ups and downs.

Writers face the same peaks, and valleys with one exception. Writers create the struggles and triumphs of people or characters that don't exist and carry the reader down the path with them. Writers live in two worlds, the real one and an imaginary one. Non-fiction writers aren't living in an imaginary world but they still live in a world of education and information. Both types of writers deal with the desire to find approval from their editors, publishers, and readers. They also want the approval of their peers. Most writers hold down a job, have family obligations, church or spiritual responsibilities, and normal life routines, in addition to being a writer. That's a lot.

Sometimes obligations or responsibilities weigh more heavily, and life is interrupted by difficult circumstances. Your job may require you to work overtime, or your hours may be cut in a slow season, causing financial crunches. An aging parent needs more help, or a spouse or child suddenly faces a dire or chronic illness. You may become ill. These seasons can choke the creative mind. Life is filled with worry, weeping, mourning, and even death. These times are hard and can overwhelm us. These times are also temporary.

My mother died several years ago. Those first few years, I could not think of her without tears. I can still have those tears today, but after some time passed, I could remember the joys of my mother and talk about her without defaulting to tears. My mother never wanted us to hang over her grave and cry daily for her. She wanted us to move on and live a good life. The day of her death and for a long time after, it was a time to mourn and weep. I can still shed those same tears today, but the days to mourn or weep are over.

What do those times of darkness mean to me? I have suffered from illness and injuries that caused worry, fear, and weariness. I've lost jobs, a house to fire, dealt with aging relatives, nearly declared bankruptcy, and much more. These dark times have offered me insight into emotions, helped me grow in my faith, and served to create a sense of thankfulness.

If everything was good all the time, we would become complacent like the children of Israel did so many times and fall into sin. I'm not suggesting that God allows bad things to happen to us simply to keep us in line. In Matthew 5:45(NKJV) Jesus says that God, "...makes his sun rise on the evil and on the good, and sends rain on the just and on the unjust." Tough times are going to happen, but so are good times. Having the good times, makes it easier to handle the bad times. Knowing that God is there no matter what we're facing gets us through the difficult times. Our ability to praise and worship him is enhanced by both the good and the bad. We are thankful when he gives us the good times and grateful when he brings us out of the bad times.

How does this play into writing? If the story of Snow White didn't have an evil queen, it might have been a rather dull story. Writing stories, or using real-life examples in non-fiction stories, captures the reader. Those difficult times that we face can be used to recreate emotions in what we write, making it richer and fuller. This is true for both fiction and non-fiction. The difficult times we face, even if they aren't exactly like the stories we create, can help us convey the story's emotion to our readers.

Use your own trials and temptations to write a vivid rising action, climax, and falling action. You can also use those events to help a friend through a difficult time. It's easier to know what someone needs when you've been through a relatable circumstance.

Reading is done for education, escape from reality, or inspiration. If my problems are so great that I need to read to get away from them, it is the writer's job to give me an exciting place to go. A place where, for at least a few minutes, I can be a hero, or a princess. A place of hopes and dreams that will allow me to know that whatever difficulties I am dealing with will end.

A happy life doesn't prevent one from enjoying the dream of being a superhero, a space traveler, a pioneer in the old west, or a fairy princess. They may like to explore the "what if's." Sparking the imagination with the impossible can open the door to "new" possibles. That very first verse in Ecclesiastes 3 says that there is a time for everything and every activity. There's a time to be real and a time to be imaginary. Life isn't all sadness and mourning. There are times of laughter, dancing, and reaping the harvest. Having only all good or only all bad makes for a dull or dreary story. Even in the dreary times, like Paul and Silas in the jail after suffering a painful beating, they prayed and sang praises to the Lord. I don't know how good their singing was, but they broke the jail.

Ecclesiastes 3 is about hope and believing that whatever we're going through, it is temporary. God knew about it before you ever got there and he knows the way out, so even in the dark times, laugh and dance. Psalm 30:5 "For his anger lasts only a moment, but his favor lasts a lifetime; weeping may stay for the night, but rejoicing comes in the morning."

A character in my books tells her grandson that when times get tough, you can laugh or you can cry, but laughing's more fun. Cry if you have to, but laugh when you can.

SONG: *Alive & Breathing* by Matt Maher

PRAYER: Father, in all things, we give praise to you. As long as we have breath, we will praise your Holy name.

Darkness

The people walking in darkness have seen a great light; on those living in the land of deep darkness a light has dawned.
Isaiah 9:2

DARKNESS. WHAT IS DARKNESS? Darkness is the absence of light. Think about that for a moment. We have flashlights, lamps, candles, and other light generating fixtures. We don't have anything to generate darkness. If we want darkness, we have to shut out the light.

Adam and Eve were walking with God in the garden. They were walking with the one who created light, yet they traded that light for darkness. Their sin ushered darkness into the world.

Knowledge and righteousness are equated with light. When things are going well for us, we enjoy the light and the good times. A day of sunshine is considered a good day.

Sin, shame, guilt, and ignorance are equated with darkness. When things go wrong in our lives, we say that we are in a dark place or going through a dark time because we cannot see a way out of our troubles.

There is never a time so dark as when we feel like God has abandoned us and does not hear our prayers. Those times are often referred to as the "dark night of the soul".

Matthew 27:45-46 talks about Jesus' crucifixion. There was a darkness that came over all the land and Jesus himself cries out, asking God why he has forsaken him. Jesus paid the price for all the sin of all of mankind, past, present, and future. He bore all of mankind's ugliness and separation from God in those moments. The scriptures tell us that the darkness during the crucifixion began around noon and lasted for three hours, ending about the time he died. That's a moment I would love to have seen. The temple veil, which was at least four inches thick, is torn in two, the earth quakes, tombs break open, dead people come to life (Matthew 27:50-53), and the darkness is vanquished.

Jesus knew that his death was squarely within the Father's will. He knew he had done nothing wrong. He resisted Satan's temptations and remained without sin or blame, yet God's presence was obstructed by the darkness of what he was experiencing.

There are times in our own lives when darkness can hide the light from us. Sickness, financial problems, relationship problems, emotional struggles, psychological infirmities, satanic attacks, and many other things can block the light. The light isn't gone, but our vision is obstructed. A basketball is certainly not bigger than the sun, but if you hold it up in front of your face, it will block the sun from your sight. The sun hasn't left the sky, but you can't see it. Sometimes the problem is that we close our own eyes, not wanting to see the light. Self can be the biggest cause of living in darkness. We want our own way, not God's way.

Isaiah 9:2 was one of the first verses Jesus quoted when he began his ministry. All of humanity had been living under the curse of sin, death, and darkness. His death and resurrection brought light back into the world. When we face those dark times and it seems like our prayers reach no higher than the ceiling, remember that the light isn't gone. It's still there. Faith is often the only thing we have to face the darkness. Feelings are misleading. Facts aren't always helpful or factual. Faith is the evidence of things we cannot see. It is the hope we cling to in the darkness.

What does this have to do with writing, you may ask? It is often hard to write when your brain is scrambled by the darkness. I can't say specifically what God wants you to do in those dark times and nor should I—it is not my place. Do consider that there is a time for everything and this may be a time to journal whatever journey you are traversing. It might be time to stop writing for awhile. This might be the time to write the darkest things you've ever written. As I have said many times already, pray first. God hears your prayers even if it doesn't seem like it. Daniel said a prayer and his answer took twenty-one days to reach him (Daniel 10:12-14). Some answers take even longer.

Just because we can't see the light doesn't mean it isn't there. And of course, ask for the prayers and counsel of solid Christian prayer warriors. If Jesus can feel like God has forsaken him, it isn't unexpected that we might feel it too (Matthew 27:45-46).

SONG: *My Light* by Colton Dixon

PRAYER: Jesus, help us to remember that you are the light that shines in the darkness and that the darkness has not overcome you.

Spiritual Attacks

The Lord will rescue me from every evil attack and will bring me safely to his heavenly kingdom. To him be glory for ever and ever. Amen.
2 Timothy 4:18

EVERY TRUE CHRISTIAN faces spiritual battles. Spiritual battles are not the same as trials and tribulations, although those may be present as well. The more effective we are as disciples for Christ, the more likely we are to face spiritual attacks.

Eve fought in the first spiritual battle in the Garden of Eden and lost. Satan tempted her, not with a piece of fruit, but with doubt. "Did God really say...?"

The first step to fixing a problem is to recognize that you have one. How do we recognize the attacks of Satan or one of his followers? Satan's voice causes chaos, doubt, fear, condemnation, pushes you to make rash decisions, and turns contemplation into worry. God's voice brings peace, comfort, reassurance. He will lead you and sometimes he will discipline and convict you, but his presence during those situations will still be loving. Satan's voice accuses and judges.

Isaiah 54:17 says, "no weapon forged against you will prevail, and you will refute every tongue that accuses you. This is the heritage of the servants of the Lord, and this is their vindication from me, declares the Lord." This verse tells us that weapons against us will fail.

First, we will be attacked. Satan has weapons, and he's certainly not afraid to use them against us. Second, we have the power to refute the accusations of our enemy. It is our heritage from the Lord. When we were redeemed we were vindicated, cleared, pardoned, and forgiven. Satan can accuse us all he wants, but the slate is wiped clean. Satan can bring up every little thing we've done wrong, but Jesus, the one whose opinion matters, sees the blank slate.

There is a scene in the movie, *Thumbelina* where Thumbelina tells Jacquimo that the beetle said she was ugly. Jacquimo, in his French accent, wisely asks, "Do you love ze beetle?" To which she replies, "No." And he responds with, "Zen nevermind ze beetle."

If we don't love Satan, then his opinion of us is irrelevant. In 2 Timothy, the Lord promises to rescue us from every evil attack. He will transport us safely to his heavenly kingdom. In Matthew 10:28, Jesus tells us not to be afraid of those who can kill the body, but to be afraid of the one who can destroy the body and the soul. He's talking about God, not Satan. Satan can tempt us, push us, and provoke us, but ultimately, it is God who judges us.

Fear can be a tool of Satan, but it is also a tool that protects us. If you are afraid of falling, you are not likely to climb out onto a ledge. The nerves in our body warn us of things that can harm us, like illness or injury. A healthy fear protects us from making poor decisions. An unhealthy fear paralyzes us.

Fear, worry, doubt, confusion, and discouragement will happen to all of us. How we handle them is the moment when we face our attacker and surrender to him or fight him. If we give in to fears or doubts and stop moving forward, we lose our battle. If we stand firm and don't give these things a foothold in our lives, even if our worst fears come true, we haven't lost our battle.

Ephesians chapter 6 gives us a list of weapons and protective gear. The breastplate of righteousness is that clean slate mentioned earlier. The belt of truth gives us that voice to refute the accuser's lies. The gospel of peace protects our feet so that we may stand our ground. The shield of faith protects us from not just ordinary arrows, but flaming arrows. We are to wear the helmet of salvation and take up the word of God as the sword of the Spirit.

Satan can be very subtle in his attacks. First it's a small whisper of doubt or fear, then another, and another, and suddenly you are floundering in the ocean like Peter when he stepped out of the boat. Peter had the courage to step out and we often do, too. But when he was too far to get back in, and Jesus was still beyond his reach, his fear took over and he dropped his shield of faith. Jesus' first words to Peter were, "You of little faith, why did you doubt?"

My first large spiritual battle as a writer was doubting that God actually called me to do this. I spent months, even years, off and on hearing the words "Did God really say..." Once I recognized those words from Genesis, I knew who was speaking to me and why. Satan doesn't need to attack the complacent, or the rebellious because they aren't listening to God's instruction. I may not be Billy Graham, John Wesley, Martin Luther, or the Apostle Paul and my reach is certainly not as large as theirs, but I am a servant of the Most High God and a child of The King. When I write, it is to share God's love for me and others, whether it is through a fictional story or an inspirational non-fiction book.

The Christian singer, Carmen, wrote a song many years ago called, "Not 4 Sale." It talks about Satan trying to tempt him to sing for the secular world instead of for Christ. In the song, he is promised wealth and fame so long as he doesn't support the name of Jesus. I suspect there are things I could write that might make me a fortune, but they wouldn't be pleasing to God, so I'm not writing those things. When I am under attack, it may take a little time for me to realize what is happening. But when I put things into perspective, I realize that battle I'm in is meant to paralyze me with fear and stop my progress.

When the world feels like it's caving in around you, or the waves wash over your head and you begin to sink into the depths of the sea, recognize it for the attack that it is. Pray first and enlist the prayers of others. Ready your weapons and armor. Remember 2 Timothy 4:18, he will rescue us from every evil attack. In Deuteronomy, he promises never to leave us or forsake us. When we are in the heat of battle, we are not alone. The Lord is with us, whether it is a physical trial or a spiritual one. Don't entertain the doubts and fears. They only lead to more doubts and fears. To be tempted is not a sin, but to dwell on and entertain that temptation brings us to the point of sin. To have a doubt or a fear is expected. Giving those things control over you is when we start losing the battle.

SONGS: *Fear is a Liar* by Zach Williams and *Battle Belongs* Phil Wickham

PRAYER: Lord Jesus, help us recognize your voice and listen only to you. Remind us to cast all our cares on you and stop holding onto them ourselves.

Be Strong and Courageous

"Be strong and very courageous. Be careful to obey all the law my servant Moses gave you; do not turn from it to the right or to the left, that you may be successful wherever you go. Keep this Book of the Law always on your lips; meditate on it day and night, so that you may be careful to do everything written in it. Then you will be prosperous and successful. Have I not commanded you? Be strong and courageous. Do not be afraid; do not be discouraged, for the Lord your God will be with you wherever you go."

Joshua 1:7-9

IN JOSHUA 1:7-9, THE Israelites were about to enter the Promised Land. No doubt this new generation remembered their parents' tales of woe over the giants inhabiting the land and God's displeasure with them over their refusal to enter the land. This passage is God speaking to Joshua, telling him to be strong and courageous. He isn't talking to the children of Israel, but to Joshua, of all people. Joshua was the one who, forty years earlier, said, "Let's go. We can take them." Why did Joshua need to hear such an admonition?

Joshua had been at Moses' side for the last forty years in the thick of things. He was with the Israelites when they left Egypt, saw every miracle, and knew how stiff-necked and rebellious the people were.

The children of Israel spent forty years in the desert growing strong, having their faith established and built up, and gaining a reputation for being a formidable adversary. God's presence among his people was apparent when the Israelites won battles they shouldn't have won.

With the death of Moses, God's chosen leader, would the people follow Joshua with the same dedication and trust? Would God leave them when Moses died? Was Joshua afraid?

Many times we second-guess ourselves if we don't hear a specific word from God. The day I wrote this, I was second-guessing myself on other matters. It's easy to do, but we cannot give into doubt and fear. I had doubts that God had really called me to write and it took a long time to put that fear to rest. Fear, doubt, and discouragement are Satan's weapons. God gave Joshua a recipe for success. In the verses prior, Joshua is told to study, meditate on, and obey the Mosaic laws—and tells him twice to be strong and courageous. He also tells him not to be afraid or discouraged. Why? Because the Lord his God would be with him wherever he went.

Christianity is not popular in this world. Jesus warned his disciples that the world would hate them because it hated him first. Writing anything Christian in the climate of book banning and anti-Christian sentiments is risky. In the current societal and political climates, taking a stand and labeling sin as sin can create a fearful and discouraging backlash. Just as God commanded Joshua to obey the laws of Moses and not to stray, we have to do the same thing. We have to do what is right in God's sight, even when it's scary. Peter was crucified, Stephen was stoned, and even today, many are martyred for their Christian beliefs. If you feel God has called you to write something, then write it. Be strong and courageous. Don't be afraid or discouraged. God will be with you wherever you go.

SONG: *God Leads His Dear Children Along* performed by Selah and *I Will Fear No More* by The Afters

PRAYER: God, give us the strength and courage to do what you have called us to do, remembering that you are with us, wherever we go.

Who I Am vs. What I Do

I am the vine; you are the branches. If you remain in me and I in you, you will bear much fruit; apart from me you can do nothing...This is to my Father's glory, that you bear much fruit, showing yourselves to be my disciples."
John 15:5, 8

AS A WRITER, WHEN WE create a book, story, novel, poem, etc., a piece of our heart, minds, and even souls goes into it. In the novels I have written, I see myself, my relationship with my husband, and the desires of my heart. No, I am not a starship captain, but I have some of the same care and compassion as the characters I created. This raises the question, "If I am not a starship captain, who am I?"

In John 15, Jesus puts our identity into perspective. Jesus is the true vine and God the Father is the gardener. We have a great attachment to the books that we write. They are a part of us. We are a branch that is connected to the vine and fed by the vine. The books we write are the fruits produced when we are supplied nutrients by the true vine. A fruit bears the same basic genetic structure as the plant that produces it. If you take the seeds from that fruit, it will produce another plant of the same variety. The seeds from a cucumber do not produce a squash, and the seeds from an apple tree don't produce peach trees.

The fruit of a tree or vine can provide sustenance or seeds that can be planted to produce a new fruit-bearing plant (genetic manipulation aside). The fruit, although it bears a genetic resemblance to the plant, is not the plant.

You are a branch and the fruit you produce comes from being connected to Jesus, the true vine. Writing books and stories flows from the love for the Savior. He calls us his children, his friends, his disciples, and members of his body. The beauty and wonder of his redemption of us blossoms into a flower, and, when pollinated, forms a fruit (or vegetable).

When the fruit is plucked in season from the branch, the branch is not harmed. The branch continues to bear fruit. If someone takes a bite of the fruit and it isn't to their liking, they may toss it away. As a writer, someone may read my written work and not like it. It's disappointing when that happens, but it will happen. Someone else may take a bite and devour the fruit, loving every bite. You are not the fruit; you are the branch. If someone doesn't like the fruit you produce, you will still be a branch and produce more fruit in each season.

It hurts when somebody doesn't like our writing because it is a piece of us. Further down in John 15, Jesus says that if the world hates you, it's because we aren't a part of the world. We are a part of Christ and the world hated Christ. If someone doesn't like your writing, maybe it's not their preferred genre—or maybe—it's because your writing represents Christ and they hate him. Maybe if the work you labor and sweat over isn't liked, or is hated, it is because you did it right. The enemy recognizes God's gardening and Christ's lifeblood. Don't let someone's distaste for your work make you feel like a failure or think poorly of yourself. You are not the fruit; you are the branch. We don't have control over what people do with the fruit, but know that God is using you to produce fruit.

SONG: *Fingerprints of God* by Steven Curtis Chapman

PRAYER: Father, on the third day, you created plants to bear fruit and seeds after its kind and you said it was good. May the fruit we bear come only from you.

Validation

The angel of the Lord came back a second time and touched him and said, "Get up and eat, for the journey is too much for you." So he got up and ate and drank. Strengthened by that food, he traveled forty days and forty nights until he reached Horeb, the mountain of God. There he went into a cave and spent the night. And the word of the Lord came to him: "What are you doing here, Elijah?" He replied, "I have been very zealous for the Lord God Almighty. The Israelites have rejected your covenant, torn down your altars, and put your prophets to death with the sword. I am the only one left, and now they are trying to kill me too."
I Kings 19:7-10

THIS PASSAGE IN I KINGS occurs after several big events in the life of Elijah. God had given Elijah a message for Ahab that a drought was coming. After a three-year successful fulfillment of that prophecy and an unrepentant King, Elijah challenges the King and his prophets of Baal and Asherah to a showdown on Mount Carmel. After a long day of watching the King's prophets making fools of themselves, Elijah prepares a sacrifice of his own to God and invites God to prove himself to the people of Israel. God proved himself with room to spare by accepting the offering and ending the drought.

God handed Elijah a great victory. Things can go great for a time and we often ride high after our victories, but one thing can cause us to stumble. Queen Jezebel wasn't happy that Elijah was responsible for the death of her prophets. She began a manhunt to destroy him and promised him he would be dead by the next evening. Elijah ran for his life. He reached a point of depression right after an amazing victory. He went into the wilderness and prayed to die.

Did God take his life? No, God sent an angel to feed him. God ministered to his physical needs. He didn't chastise him. God strengthened and sustained him, then sent him in a new direction.

What happened next? God asked Elijah what he was doing hiding in the cave. Do you think God didn't know every thought and feeling Elijah was experiencing?

God knew. So why did he ask?

I was suffering a bit of angst over a medical procedure some years ago. God asked me to write down everything I was worried about regarding the procedure. I did as he asked and made my list. After I finished, I presented my list back to him. God then asked me to point to the one I thought he couldn't handle. Talk about feeling foolish. It wasn't God's purpose to make me feel foolish, but to help me realize that I was worrying needlessly. He already knew the answers. Now he was showing me the answers. I suspect that was part of his purpose with Elijah.

Elijah told God he had been doing what God wanted but was distraught that the Israelites were still rejecting God. How many times are we in the center of God's will, but feel like things aren't going right? How many times do we doubt what we are doing, the way we are doing it, and whether we should be the ones doing it? Surely there's somebody better, right? God knows how to put the right person in the right place at the right time. Are we doubting ourselves or God's judgment? Moses offered God a lot of excuses for not facing down Pharaoh and leading the children of Israel out of Egypt. God knew every excuse Moses was going to offer so much that he told Moses that his brother Aaron was already on his way to meet him. *Already on his way.*

When we write, we are putting a piece of ourselves out there and exposing every nerve in our being. It's easy to question what we're doing. Did God really call me to be a writer? Is this what I'm supposed to be writing? Did I use the right method to publish? That's doubt.

Elijah didn't actually doubt what God told him to do, but doubted the effectiveness of it. He had this great victory proving God was God, but not much changed. Did God stop moving forward? No, God appointed new leaders to keep the mission moving forward—and Elijah was still part of the plan.

Validation may come in many forms. Elijah stood at the mouth of that cave, waiting for the Lord. God wasn't in the strong wind. He wasn't in the earthquake or the fire. He was in the still, small voice. Elijah recognized his Lord's voice. Sometimes God gives us a big bold sign like Mount Carmel and sometimes he speaks through the whispers.

We may not see the end results of what we do when we serve the Lord. How many lives have been changed by Gideon Bibles in a hotel room? How many lives have been changed by a children's Sunday School teacher or the pastor of a tiny backwoods church? We may not know this side of eternity. We aren't the mission; God is. Sometimes, like with Elijah, when things go wrong, it's because we're doing it right.

Hold on to what you know to be true and let God work out the rest of the plan. There's no god like Jehovah and no plans like his plans.

SONG: *Days of Elijah* by various artists

PRAYER: Father, give us the faith in what we hope for and the assurance of the things we don't see.

The Apostle's Job

And God has placed in the church first of all apostles
I Corinthians 12: 28

AN APOSTLE IS SOMEONE sent on a mission to preach the gospel. While writers may or may not view themselves as apostles, Christians should consider themselves apostles. The Great Commission, "to go and make disciples of all nations" is addressed to all of us. How we enact that mandate varies. Some quietly witness by their actions and others proclaim Christ loudly. Writers share their faith in similar variations.

Nonfiction books on discipleship, inspirational stories, or devotional stories are more direct in sharing the gospel and encouraging spiritual growth. Fiction books with a Christian theme or allegory are less direct, but evident. Clean fiction with no spiritual theme provides an alternative to the secular world's options. It may not build one up spiritually, but it won't tear you down.

If you choose to use your writing to build a believer's faith or to witness to an unbeliever, you are acting in the role of an apostle. The apostle Paul ranks apostles as the highest of spiritual appointments and encourages us to strive for the greater gifts, which includes apostleship.

There have been many times I have heard personal testimonies that have strengthened my faith and walk with the Lord. Whether I share verbatim a time in my life where the Lord has helped me through a particular situation or if I create a similar fictitious circumstance, I am sharing God's love for us.

King David was known as a man after God's own heart. If you love the Lord with all your heart, you will want to learn all that you can about him. You'll spend time in God's Word, spend time praying, or—in other terms—talking with him. You'll reach a point where you can't live your life without him.

I don't know if you've noticed or not, but I don't end my prayers at the bottom of the devotional with "amen." The reason I did this is because we are to "pray without ceasing" (I Thessalonians 5:17 NKJV) and I want to encourage you to not leave God in your corner where you have your time of dedication and devotion. Don't stop praying just because you leave your "prayer closet." If you can't live without him, you'll take him with you to the store, work, and everywhere you go.

When you are at that point, you will gladly share his love for you in any way you can. We are still limited in what we can do, and we can't be all things to all people—nor should we. If you desire to share God's love through your writing, that is the behavior of an apostle. It isn't the same as someone who is speaking verbally, but it *is* speaking through written words.

There are some who believe apostles are limited to the first twelve or only twelve. Paul was not one of the first twelve, but Romans chapter one says, "Paul, a servant of Christ Jesus, called to be an apostle...." In chapter sixteen of Romans, Paul refers to Andronicus and Junia as apostles. In I Corinthians 4, Paul gives a rather graphic description of the apostles. He says he and the other apostles are a spectacle put on display, and are fools for Christ. They go hungry and thirsty, wear rags, don't have homes, and they are slandered. The NIV in verse 13 says, "We have become the scum of the earth, the garbage of the world..." Although we may not view ourselves as apostles, how many of us make a living at writing? How many of us have received a slanderous book review for showing our Christian faith in our books?

The apostles were men who used the power of God to heal the sick, raise the dead, and discerned truth from those who would try to deceive them. As writers, we don't usually display that sort of power, but we can help those who are sick or grieving to weather the storm by giving them stories that lift their spirits and distract them from the pain of the moment. We can write non-fiction books about the struggles of chronic illness or dealing with grief.

Whether we ever reach a point where we are considered apostles or not isn't really the issue. We are to strive for that point. We are to love God and want to share him with others so much that it invades all that we do. To be an apostle of Christ is to follow him in every aspect of our lives and with every ounce of our being. The same God who empowered the prophets in the Old Testament and the apostles in the New Testament is the same God today. He is the source of our strength. We love and serve the same God as Moses, David, and Paul. He loves us just as much as he loved them. You serve the God who raised Christ, and others, from the dead. He is the same God who led the children of Israel through the sea on dry ground. He protected the children of Israel from numerous annihilations and gave children to a one hundred-year-old man. He is still caring for his children today and he's using you to do it.

SONG: *Same God* by Elevation Worship

PRAYER: Heavenly Father, give us the desire to follow you as deeply as you would have us go.

Getting Overwhelmed

Then Jesus went with his disciples to a place called Gethsemane, and he said to them, "Sit here while I go over there and pray."
He took Peter and the two sons of Zebedee along with him, and he began to be sorrowful and troubled. Then he said to them, "My soul is overwhelmed with sorrow to the point of death. Stay here and keep watch with me."
Going a little farther, he fell with his face to the ground and prayed, "My Father, if it is possible, may this cup be taken from me. Yet not as I will, but as you will."
Matthew 26: 36-39

GETTING OVERWHELMED means hitting a point where we are no longer in control. Sometimes that is a good thing and sometimes it isn't, but it happens to all of us. Strong emotions can impair reason and understanding for a time.

In Mark 7:37, the people who were watching and following Jesus were overwhelmed at all the miracles Jesus was performing. In the book of Job, Job was overwhelmed by the downward turn his life took and he had no explanation why things had gone this way. He had done everything right he knew to do. In the books of I & II Samuel and I Kings, King David was overwhelmed by his enemies and by his circumstances—although he generally knew why the events were happening to him. Sometimes they were caused by his own poor choices and other times they weren't.

There's another important example of someone who was overwhelmed. Jesus was overwhelmed with sorrow.

When we get overwhelmed, we are usually in the middle of a crisis. There are deadlines looming in front of us, demands for our time and attention, and emergencies popping up out of nowhere. Jesus wasn't quite in the middle of the situation yet. He had time to walk away. His situation differed from ours because he knew what was coming and he knew the stakes. Do we handle our circumstances differently? Jesus took his disciples, his closest friends to Gethsemane and prayed.

Our Heavenly Father can see how we got into the mess we're in and he can see the way out. Jesus was both human and the Son of God. He felt pain both physically and emotionally. In Gethsemane, he was sorrowful and troubled. The physical pain hadn't begun yet. He was troubled about his upcoming appointment with death and the temptation(s) his disciples would face. There was a lot on his plate. He was about to pay the price for the sin of all of humanity. He became sin, which is detestable to God and separates us from the Heavenly Father. If anyone had a reason to be overwhelmed; it was Jesus.

When we reach a point of being overwhelmed, reason may not be our closest companion. Having the support of friends and companions can help us put things into perspective. Prayer is also crucial. There are times when I have been overwhelmed and can't even form sentences. My prayers at times like that resemble those of a child bringing a broken toy to their father, tearfully holding it up and saying, "Daddy, fix it."

Jesus *kept his friends close* and *took his needs to his Father*. He *separated himself from all other distractions*. The last thing he did was *accept his circumstances as being God's will*. His circumstances were short-lived. They were hard to go through even though he had the authority to call 10,000 angels to come to his aid.

Job didn't have the power to call 10,000 angels. David didn't have the authority either, but both continued to serve the Lord and seek his face in the middle of their circumstances. Their situations were temporary. God didn't leave them overwhelmed and at the mercy of their circumstances. Sometimes we need to take our circumstances and just sit at the feet of Jesus and let his peace overwhelm our circumstances.

SONG: *The More I Seek You* by Kari Jobe

PRAYER: Father, help us remember that you are bigger than our circumstances.

God's Timing

But those who wait on the Lord Shall renew their strength; They shall mount up with wings like eagles, They shall run and not be weary, They shall walk and not faint.
Isaiah 40:31 (NKJV)

THE WORD "TIME" IN various forms is mentioned 888 times in the NIV. God has a lot to say about time. God is not bound by time; we are. When God created man, he already knew what troublemakers we would be. Thousands of years before Christ was born, he gave us prophecies to help us identify the Messiah when he arrived. God puts people in the right places at the right time repeatedly in scripture.

In Esther 4, Mordecai tells Esther that perhaps she was put into the position of being Queen at that specific time for the purpose of saving her people.

Joseph went through many troubling times to become the second highest power in Egypt. His position allowed him to save his family and many others from death during the seven years of famine.

When the Ethiopian was reading and not understanding the book of Isaiah, God sent Philip to explain it to him. The Ethiopian didn't know he needed help, but God provided it.

The problem with God's timing is we get our eyes set on our own circumstances and lose focus on God. When Peter stepped out of the boat, he walked on the water until he took his eyes off the Savior. He wasn't close enough to reach Jesus, and he wasn't close enough to get back in the boat, but Jesus was at his side just in time.

When we pray, we want the answer—right now! God might give us the answer right now, or he may not. Isaiah 40:31 says those who *wait*... Wait—not act impulsively or throw a temper tantrum—will have renewed strength and soar to great heights.

Many writers are juggling jobs, families, and other responsibilities with their writing. Finances are a struggle. If you self-publish, finding the money for an editor or a book cover can stress your finances. If you publish traditionally, finding the right publisher or agent at the right time when your particular genre is trending can take time, and it's hard to wait.

When I published my first book, I was excited to be so close to seeing the fruition of years of labor. I moved too fast and made mistakes.

Waiting on God is never easy. We see the waves crashing around us and we lose our focus. God knows what's ahead of us and he knows what's best for us. Of course, waiting on the Lord involves that big, bad, ugly word known as "Patience." Does that word make your hair stand on end?

While we wait on God, we need to look at the times he's supplied our needs. Look at the past victories and struggles. If you are new to Christianity and don't have those past victories, listen to someone else's victories, read about the victories in scripture.

Another thing we need to be prepared to accept is that sometimes he says "no" to the answer we have asked for. We may think that a new "job opportunity" is a dream come true, but at the time we didn't know the company was about to be bought out and the new owner would lay off half the employees.

Esau came in famished, begging his brother for a bowl of stew. Isaac had large flocks and herds. Did Esau not have the strength to milk a goat, or a servant to milk the goat for him? Esau didn't have patience and if he had been that sickly, even though Jacob was Rebekah's favorite, what mother would have ignored her son's desperate need? No, Esau didn't wait. He was impatient, and it cost him his birthright.

I Peter 5:7 says, "Cast all your anxiety on him because he cares for you." God has a plan and his timing is not our timing—and his timing is amazing. I've thought for years that I needed to write a devotional, but the timing was never right until now and even before this was published, it was bearing fruit. God is never early, and he's never late.

I HAVE TWO SONGS FOR you today.

Songs: *While I'm Waiting* by John Waller, and *Help Is On The Way* by Toby Mac

PRAYER: Lord Jesus, remind us that things happen according to your plan and are resolved according to your timetable, not ours.

Burnout

Then he told them many things in parables, saying: "A farmer went out to sow his seed. As he was scattering the seed, some fell along the path, and the birds came and ate it up. Some fell on rocky places, where it did not have much soil. It sprang up quickly, because the soil was shallow. But when the sun came up, the plants were scorched, and they withered because they had no root. Other seed fell among thorns, which grew up and choked the plants. Still other seed fell on good soil, where it produced a crop—a hundred, sixty or thirty times what was sown.
Matthew 13: 3-8

BURNOUT. THAT'S THE feeling you get when you don't want to do something anymore. Burnout can happen when we've lost our joy in a certain activity. You can reach that point with writing. How do you get there? One minute you're writing exciting tales of imaginary worlds or relating real tales of actual life events. They are good tales whether they are real or imaginary, so how did you get burned out?

It's a genuine problem. You have publishing deadlines that are coming fast and hard whether they are self-imposed or imposed from outside, whether you're trying to write to market or write to your own preferences. There isn't anything wrong with either one, but it still increases stress and pressure. Perhaps someone important has disapproved of what you are doing, a loved one feels you are wasting your life, or that fairies can't be Christians. The reasons for writer burnout are just as extensive as burnout for other tasks. Frequent criticism, unrealistic expectations, schedule interruptions, or not getting the satisfaction and success you expected can all cause burnout.

Jesus told the parable of the seeds and the soils. When the farmer scattered the seeds, some fell on rocky soil, some on the hard path, some among the thorns, and some on good ground. If you are familiar with gardening, you know weeds will crop up even in the good ground. Weeds actually like it there because the soil is fertile. In order to stay fertile, you have to keep your field clear of those unwanted thieves. Having weeds and thorns doesn't make the soil bad, but it does hinder the growth and harvest. A harvest takes a lot of work. From tilling the soil, planting the seeds, watering, fertilizing, pulling weeds, and finally reaping what you sowed can be tiring. It's the same with writing.

You build your world, create your characters, outline your story (if you are a plotter), write your draft, proof, edit, proof, edit, proof, edit, format, design your cover, write your blurb, edit, proof, market, and publish. If you have a traditional publisher, you can take out one set of those proofs and edits, most of the cover designing, the formatting, and the blurb. That's still a lot of work. When the load gets too heavy, it's time to find the weeds.

In the practical world, when you realize you are burned out, it's time to do some re-evaluation. Is your schedule too full? Does something need to be slowed down or eliminated? Do deadlines need to be moved? Is a particular project weighing you down? Perhaps it's time to lay that one aside or get some help with it.

In Isaiah 40, it says that even the young will get tired and weary, even the young will stumble and fall, but that's not the end. There is renewal of strength when we hope in the Lord. Jesus invites us to come to him. When we get overloaded and lose the joy we had in writing, we need to go to Jesus and learn from him. He'll teach us what he wants us to know.

Before making any decisions, pray. Ask God for his guidance. Galatians 6:9 says, "Let us not become weary in doing good, for at the proper time we will reap a harvest if we do not give up." God promises a harvest if we don't give up.

SONG: *Breathe* by Jonny Diaz

PRAYER: Jesus, take the weeds from my garden and leave only the harvest you provided. Refresh and strengthen me. Renew my joy.

Staying Focused

As Jesus and his disciples were on their way, he came to a village where a woman named Martha opened her home to him. She had a sister called Mary, who sat at the Lord's feet listening to what he said. But Martha was distracted by all the preparations that had to be made. She came to him and asked, "Lord, don't you care that my sister has left me to do the work by myself? Tell her to help me!"

"Martha, Martha," the Lord answered, "you are worried and upset about many things, but few things are needed—or indeed only one. Mary has chosen what is better, and it will not be taken away from her."

Luke 10:38-42

WRITERS HAVE THE SAME life as other people. Writers typically have jobs, family responsibilities, church obligations, and hobbies, plus the added task of writing. Writers are thinkers. Their minds can run ninety miles an hour while sitting still. They are plotting the next chapter in their book at the same time they are thinking about the appointments and deadlines on their calendar—and of course, the prayer requests they heard at Bible Study. Then on to decide what to eat for dinner. This child has a ballgame, that one has dance lessons, choir practice is at seven and dinner will have to be drive-thru. By the time the nightly race has been run, the kids are in bed, and homework is done, do you have the strength to write, have your own devotional time, prayer, or even a quiet conversation with your spouse?

In the hubbub of life, it's easy to forget what's important. It's easy to say I'm too busy or tired to spend time with Jesus. Jesus will understand, won't he? We can skip one appointed devotional time with him, then another, and a third, and suddenly it's been a week and we're feeling empty—and this is if everything is going normally.

What happens when one child catches the flu, the car breaks down, a summons for jury duty shows up in the mail, and the in-laws want to come for a visit? Nothing against in-laws, I love mine very much, but it does raise the stress level a bit to have visitors even if they are family. Can you stay focused on what's important now?

Things can get even more stressful and hectic when the washer decides to quit, the second child catches the flu from the first, your company decides to lay you off, and your doctor wants to do a biopsy on you. When things hit this level, just making it through the day gets difficult; forget writing.

When times are normal and hectic, we need to take the time to spend at the feet of Jesus, loving him, learning from him, and revitalizing ourselves. When things start to go awry, the first place we need to go is to the one who controls all things. He is the one who can control what we can't. Yes, you may have to adapt to your circumstances, like having your Bible read aloud to you via a phone app while you shower, eat breakfast, or drive to work. Take a moment to kneel before the King of Kings that designed everything from sub-atomic particles to Saturn's rings to galaxy after galaxy. When things are spinning out of control, run to his throne, remembering he is the one who set the planets to spinning in the first place.

Jesus cares for you and what you are going through. In the scripture for today, Jesus' message to Martha was that he didn't care if she was the perfect hostess. He cared about her, not tea and crumpets. When we spend time with the Lord, it doesn't mean things won't go wrong, but it keeps us close to the source we need when things *do* happen. Jesus is the reason we have the things that are in our lives. He created us, created our families, gave us our jobs, our desire and ability to write, and many more things. If you don't have those things, he still created you.

He is what fuels our lives physically, emotionally, intellectually, and spiritually. We can't glean from him if we don't spend time with him. Sit down at his feet, listen to his words, and feel his love for you. When this one area of our lives isn't in order, the rest of our life can fall into disarray. Make sure your children see you spend time with him. If those around us don't see us treasure our time with the Lord, they won't see a reason to treasure time with him either. Jesus is our creator and the one we depend on for our own creativity. He is our foundation, and if our foundation isn't stable, the whole building is crooked and can even fall apart.

The scripture doesn't say what Martha did. Did she sit down next to Mary, or did she go back to working alone? I think she sat down. I don't know if her thoughts quieted as quickly, but I'll bet she became wrapped up in Jesus' words and slowly forgot the tea and crumpets. What are you going to choose?

SONG: *Throne Room* by Kim Walker-Smith

PRAYER: Father, keep me focused on you and place the other things in life behind you.

Squandering Your Talents

"His master replied, 'You wicked, lazy servant! So you knew that I harvest where I have not sown and gather where I have not scattered seed? Well then, you should have put my money on deposit with the bankers, so that when I returned I would have received it back with interest.

"'So take the bag of gold from him and give it to the one who has ten bags. For whoever has will be given more, and they will have an abundance. Whoever does not have, even what they have will be taken from them.

Matthew 25:26-29

Recommended reading Matthew 25: 14-29

THE SCRIPTURE IN MATTHEW chapter 25 is the parable about the man who gave his servants talents or bags of gold depending on the version you are reading. He gave one servant ten bags of gold, another five and a third one was given one bag. Each one doubled their money by the time their master returned except for the third man. The third man kept the money safe and hidden away, but accomplished nothing with it.

This scripture has often been used to refer to the talents and gifts God has given each one of us. The parable in some translations uses the word "talents" which is a monetary unit. A "talent" was equal to about twenty years of pay for the average worker. It didn't technically refer to an individual's spiritual gifts, but the concept is the same.

God has given all of us resources to use and whatever he gives us should be used to further his kingdom. Some have the gift of hospitality, some have the gift of compassion, discernment, wisdom, and some are financially gifted. Whatever God has given you, he expects you to use it wisely and to use it for God's glory. If you have a gift in children's ministry and never use it, the day will come that you can't handle children anymore.

One resource that we all have is twenty-four hours a day. What do we do with those hours? Are we playing video games? Stuck on social media? Binge watching subscription television? There's nothing wrong with those things unless they become all that you do in life.

There are lots of activities that we can distract from writing. The oldest child has dance lessons, the next one has basketball practice, the third has karate lessons, and the youngest is in gymnastics. Wednesday night is church, Friday is family night, Saturday there are errands to run, the house needs cleaning, the lawn needs mowing, and the list goes on.

Unexpected occurrences can add to an already hectic schedule like a storm knocks the power out, so dinner is at a restaurant and homework doesn't get done. Your aging parents need help. These things can be exhausting and wreak havoc on routines.

There comes a point when you have to decide where to draw lines. How much is too much? God expects you to be a good steward with your time and resources. Whatever your schedule, God made the concept of a sabbath or day of rest for you and your physical, mental, and spiritual well-being. Take time to rest and keep that time set apart.

Writers often have the responsibility of a "day" job, family, church, and additional hobbies like fishing, gardening, or making crafts. How does one write in the middle of the chaos? Should you even try?

I remember when my children were young, and I got frustrated, believing I wasn't doing enough to serve God. My mother wisely told me that my job at that point in my life was to bring my children up "in the training and admonition of the Lord." (Ephesians 6:4 NKJV). Did I do any writing when the kids were young? Not a lot, but God provided the opportunities to keep my eyes focused on that goal. He also gave me experiences that expanded my learning. My life experiences have richly enhanced my writing now. Those were not wasted years of a buried talent.

If you want to write or have been called to write, but you are in a difficult season, don't abandon your gift or talent. You may need to slow down, re-prioritize, or even put it off for a time—but don't abandon your calling or God may call on someone else.

If you are in a writing season and the words are flowing, you still need to organize and pace yourself. There are drawbacks to writing too much, speaking as one who recently dealt with tennis elbow and a pinched nerve.

Consider what could have happened if the man with the five bags of gold only increased his master's money by one bag, and the second man still doubled his. Who would have gotten the bag from the slothful servant? What if the man with one bag invested the money in an unprofitable venture and lost all of it? Would his master had the same opinion of him?

Whether your gifts include writing, editing, publishing, marketing, cover art, or encouragement, use what God gave you. Jesus said whoever does this "will be given more and will have an abundance."

God has given you gifts. Don't hide them and don't hide from them. Let God guide you in how you manage your gifts and balance their use against life events. Give God control in every area of your life so that he can use you, and the talents he gave you.

SONG: *Control* by Tenth Avenue North

PRAYER: Lord, I commit my resources to you for your glory. Establish my plans according to your will.

Dealing with Attention

Instead he went out and began to talk freely, spreading the news. As a result, Jesus could no longer enter a town openly but stayed outside in lonely places. Yet the people still came to him from everywhere.
Mark 1:45

But Jesus often withdrew to lonely places and prayed.
Luke 5:16

HOW DO YOU DEAL WITH attention? Writers want to write and tell stories, but that often leads to public appearances. Many writers are also introverts who may not be comfortable around new people or crowds. A writer's conference that I have attended recognizes that, and has offered stickers for your badges to indicate that you are "talk-able."

Some people desire fame, fortune, and recognition. Others just want to quietly entertain others with a delightful tale of adventure, perhaps making a living off the proceeds. In the world of publishing and marketing, if you want your book to go anywhere, it generally requires public appearances.

In Mark chapter one, Jesus healed a leprous man but told him not to tell others about it. In his zeal, the man told everyone he could. His story spread and Jesus could no longer travel openly into the towns. His fame limited him. There were no private conversations, only throngs of needy crowds.

Famous people often travel with security guards to protect them from overzealous fans. Writers are not as visually recognized as actors or singers. We typically only have a postage stamp sized picture of us on the backs of our books.

There were no portraits of Jesus in New Testament times. Jesus was a carpenter's son, from a nothing-town in the middle of nowhere. How did he handle his fame and the throngs of people? The quick response is that he was God incarnate. He could handle anything.

After Jesus fed the five thousand plus people, he sent his disciples into a boat to cross the lake. He sent the crowds away and went up on a mountainside to pray. Luke 5:16 says that Jesus often went off by himself to pray. In his greatest hour of need, Jesus took his three closest friends near him, but stepped away from even them to pray to his Heavenly Father.

How do you deal with the attention and public appearances? Jesus didn't show any indication of struggling with public appearances. He was teaching the teachers in the temple at the age of twelve. Everyone has limits. There has to be that time to withdraw and let the dust settle.

Some may feel unworthy of the attention, be afraid of appearing in front of others, or may simply enjoy solitude. As a teenager, I was a geek and a nerd—the worst possible combination back in those days. I didn't dress right. I said all the wrong things, but I wanted desperately to be accepted and part of the crowd. A dear friend and adopted big brother wisely taught me how to be me and to stop trying to be part of the crowd.

Speaking in front of crowds can be terrifying to some people. It's hard to talk to strangers. How are they going to perceive you? Are you going to say something stupid? Being around new people can become a struggle after a time and drain one's energy levels. If you have social anxiety, this can happen very quickly.

As authors, we have to "sell" our books and ourselves. That's hard to do if you lack self-confidence, don't like talking to people, or are afraid.

If we have the self-confidence, enjoy talking to people and don't suffer from social anxiety or fear, there are still limits.

Jesus spent the forty days before his ministry began in the wilderness fasting and being tempted by Satan. Scriptures don't technically say that he prayed, but most of the time fasting accompanied prayer. He began with a time alone to focus and prepare for what he was about to do. Throughout his ministry, he took time to be alone and pray.

No matter how much you may enjoy the public eye, you have to take that time away to pray and regroup. One of the things that helps is to realize that every person you see was created by God. It doesn't mean they'll be nice to you, but it does help you to understand how to treat them. We also have to remember that we are a child of the Father and whether the public knows our name, or our face, God knows. Know who you are and who your audience is.

When dealing with the public, recognize why you are doing what you are doing. In a recent event, I was not sure what to expect. I was nervous, so I did the best thing possible. I talked about the thing I enjoyed most and that was writing stories. It's easy to talk about things you love and are excited about. Being in a secular environment, I was concerned about how much I could say from a spiritual perspective. Hours before the event, I came to terms with the fact that I write what's in my heart and that's Christian literature. If you want to know about me and my writing, that's what you will find and I'm good with that.

On a practical level, prepare answers to questions that haven't been asked. Whether you are a plotter, a pantser or somewhere in between, put together an outline of things people may want to know. Have a plan, an elevator speech, and one more important thing. If you are writing to glorify God, he's worthy of praise and honor. Our writing isn't perfect, but the one who inspires us is.

Pray first and prepare for whatever public appearance you are dealing with. Do you need downtime? Plan for it. Look at it as an opportunity to have fun and honor God. And remember that no matter what happens, God calls you his friend and his child. He knows you better than you know yourself. He will always be with you. Our own doubts and fears can make things worse than what they are. If you can't share you, share the Father.

SONG: *Who I Am* by Ben Fuller

PRAYER: Lord, my delight is in you. Make my steps firm and hold me so that I do not fall.

What Season are You In?

There is a time for everything, and a season for every activity under the heavens:
A time to be born and a time to die, a time to plant and a time to uproot,
A time to kill and a time to heal, a time to tear down and a time to build,
A time to weep and a time to laugh, a time to mourn and a time to dance,
A time to scatter stones and a time to gather them, a time to embrace and a time to refrain from embracing,
A time to search and a time to give up, a time to keep and a time to throw away,
A time to tear and a time to mend, a time to be silent and a time to speak,
A time to love and a time to hate, a time for war and a time for peace.
Ecclesiastes 3:1-8

ACCORDING TO TODAY'S scripture, there is a time to write. Granted, writing didn't technically make the list, but the first verse in Ecclesiastes 3 says, "there is a time for everything and a season for every activity."

Some people begin their writing careers as children, some as teens or young adults, and some begin later in life. There is no wrong age to begin your writing career. Each stage provides its own perspectives and strengths. Children see things simplistically and they often catch the obvious things that we as adults might miss. They ask the questions we don't think to ask. Teens and young adults often tackle the things that are hardest in life. They aren't afraid to talk about death, depression, suicide, sexuality, and other hard topics. Middle and older adults have experiences behind them that serve as a foundation to share deep feelings and hard circumstances. They've seen both happy and sad endings.

Fear is a hindrance to budding writers and there are many fears to choose from.

I'm too young to be a writer.

I don't know enough about writing.

I'm too old to start now.

I'm not like ______.

I've forgotten all those grammar rules that I learned in school.

When I went to college, my goal was to be a writer. I got busy with life and wrote almost nothing for twenty years. I was well into my forties when God redirected my life back to writing. At fifty-one, I published my first novel. I made some mistakes; it wasn't perfect. I've learned some things since then and improved it. It is much better, but it still isn't perfect and it never will be because there's always something that could be better in what we write. Looking back on the multiple novels I have published since then, I realized that the experiences I had in the twenty years of not writing have contributed a certain richness to what I've written. This is my season to write, not twenty years earlier.

God gives us seasons in our lives. Times of planting and growth, and times when the ground may lie fallow. In those times when the ground is not being tilled, something else is happening. The soil is resting and gathering nutrients for a new planting season. Just because we aren't writing at a particular time in our lives doesn't mean we aren't meant to be writers, that God is done with our writing careers, or that writing was never his plan for us. It also doesn't mean that because "John" became a writer at seventeen, we aren't meant to be writers at thirty, seventy, or ninety. Grandma Moses took up painting at the age of 78 and continued until she was 100 years old. My life is not John's life or Jane's or anyone else's. God made every one of us different and we are to live in the seasons and times he puts us in.

There is a time to write, and a time to edit. A time to create a cover, and a time to write a blurb, a time to research and a time to stop running down research rabbit holes, a time to hit "send" or "publish" and a time to refrain.

It's easy to be afraid to start, and easy to get excited and move too quickly. Take the time to pray, know what season you're in, and don't let emotion make your decisions for you.

SONG: *Seasons Change* featuring Michael Ketterer

PRAYER: God grant us the wisdom to plant in season so that we may reap a harvest that only you can provide.

Turned into Good

Then Joseph said to his brothers, "Come close to me." When they had done so, he said, "I am your brother Joseph, the one you sold into Egypt! And now, do not be distressed and do not be angry with yourselves for selling me here, because it was to save lives that God sent me ahead of you. For two years now there has been famine in the land, and for the next five years there will be no plowing and reaping. But God sent me ahead of you to preserve for you a remnant on earth and to save your lives by a great deliverance.

Genesis 45:4-7

JOSEPH'S BROTHERS ATTACKED and betrayed him. Some of them wanted to kill him. For years, they lived with the guilt of what they had done to Joseph and to their father, Jacob. They saw their father grieve the loss of his son. They saw Jacob desperately hold on to the one remaining son he had left from Rachel, the love of his life.

Joseph lived with the pain of being betrayed by his brothers. He missed his father after being separated from him for years. He did his best to survive as a slave and honor God. Potiphar's wife lied about Joseph and he lost what little position of esteem he held as a slave. Doing the right thing and ending up in prison should have pushed him into giving up, but Joseph persevered in his desire to honor God and he turned it into something good.

Everyone suffers from tragedy and hardship in their lives. There are things that while we are facing them we don't see any hope. Later, we often look back and see that God turned it into something good.

After being sold as a slave and thrown into prison, Joseph reached a new high point in his life. He was the second most powerful man in Egypt and had the approval of Pharaoh—with that came riches and power. Joseph had a wife and two sons, servants to do his bidding, and anything he wanted.

When Joseph revealed himself to the same men who rejected him, he saw their sorrowful and contrite hearts. The pain he had endured was in the past. It was over. He could have imprisoned those who hurt him and sent an envoy with Benjamin back to his father and invited him to Egypt for the duration of the famine. No one would have blamed him for seeking revenge, but he saw the situation for what it was.

God used Joseph and a painful time in his life for great and amazing things. He raised Joseph up into a prominent leader. God saved the children of Israel from extinction through a teenager's suffering. He didn't just save the Israelites. The Egyptians and the nations all around them survived.

When we write (whether it's fiction, a testimonial, a devotional, or an autobiography, or other non-fiction), we share a piece of ourselves. Our hearts and souls are revealed. I have said many times that I am a product of all of my experiences: the highs, the lows, the struggles, and the joys. When I write, I share those experiences with whoever reads what I have written. The things that were hard to face at the time become something new. Those times offer hope and encouragement to others and remind me of what God is capable of. Even in fiction works, you can find God's truth and power. I've heard critics talk about Christian works as being too sappy and too much like a fairytale. Things don't always have a happy ending. I'm sure Jesus' disciples were rattled to their core when Jesus died on that cross. Was Stephen's death a happy ending? I suppose it depends on who you ask. Stephen joined the Heavenly Father he dearly loved. The apostle Paul was there at Stephen's death, giving his approval. Was his heart and reason affected by Stephen's reaction?

Our experiences, whether written as actual events or allegory, can bring vibrancy to our writing. Whatever you are facing right now, God has a plan for it. I'm not great at journaling, but there are many times I look back and wish I had a better account of certain events in my life. Our joys and pains serve to enrich what we write. God can take the difficulties in our lives and turn them into something good, for us and for others, when we share them.

SONG: *See A Victory* by Elevation Worship.

PRAYER: Jesus, you suffered the ultimate pain for us, to give us the ultimate joy of being reunited with you. Give us the courage to turn our own pain and suffering into encouragement for others.

Don't miss out!

Visit the website below and you can sign up to receive emails whenever Reggi Broach publishes a new book. There's no charge and no obligation.

https://books2read.com/r/B-A-NTOU-ZAFPC

BOOKS 2 READ

Connecting independent readers to independent writers.

Did you love *40 Weapons of War : A Devotional for Writers*? Then you should read *Birth of the Defender* by Reggi Broach!

Two **stories, worlds** apart, yet somehow **connected.** On the backward world of **Galat**, an inconsequential planet, a young pregnant woman flees for her life. An ancient prophecy predicts the downfall of regimes with the birth of her child. The world is barely past the stone age, yet the child's birth will be felt across the galaxy.

On **Juranta**, a more advanced world, a former covert ops agent marries an accountant and daughter of two engineering geniuses. Months later, Tristan and Jessica's *child* is born—the *child* also heralded by the ancient prophecy—a prophecy his family has been forbidden to speak of.

A mysterious figure schemes to thwart the prophecies. Jessica's brother, the future admiral, Robert Deacons, witnesses the birth of the Galatan baby, and saves the lives of the infant and his mother. He suspects the child belongs to the enemy of his childhood, but he refuses to harm an innocent child. His gut tells him his enemy has already won, even if the battle hasn't started.

Robert returns to meet his newborn nephew, David Liam Alexander, a future Commonwealth captain. How are the two infants connected? What secrets bind them together? Come find out.

Read more at https://shop.reggibroach.com/.

Also by Reggi Broach

Defender Series

Birth of the Defender

The Mission

Mission Abandoned

Standalone

40 Weapons of War : A Devotional for Writers

Watch for more at https://shop.reggibroach.com/.

About the Author

Reggi Broach is the author of the *Defender Series*, a Christian Science-Fiction series of novels that follow the exploits of Captain David Alexander, Supreme Executor Luciano Hale, and the crew of the *Evangeline*. She also has several short stories that are published in anthologies with the Corner Scribblers Writing Group. Reggi graduated from Trevecca Nazarene University after studying theology, and she has graduated from Chattanooga State Community College as a registered nurse. She currently works full time as a Neonatal Intensive Care Nurse and writes any time she is not at work.

Other Work:

40 Weapons of War : A Devotional for Writer's

The Mission: Defender Series Book 1

Defended: Defender Series Book 2

Treasonous Acts: Defender Series Book 3

In Evil's Grasp: Defender Series Book 4

Mission Abandoned: Defender Series Book 5

Birth of a Revolution: Defender Series Book 6
Questions of Trust: Defender Series Book 7
Revelations: Defender Series Book 8
Sins of the Father: Defender Series Book 9
Forty Days: Defender Series Book 10
Birth of the Defender: Prequel
Take Me to Your Reader (Corner Scribblers Anthology)
Gears and Gallantry (Corner Scribblers Anthology)
In Flux, Oh Flux (Corner Scribblers Anthology)
Tales from the Street (Corner Scribblers Anthology)
Napkin Notes (Corner Scribblers Anthology)
Drunken Cranberries and other Holiday Musings (Corner Scribblers Anthology)
Dragons and Dribbles (Corner Scribblers Anthology)
Bugged Out Babblings (Corner Scribblers Anthology)
Prose and Cons (Corner Scribblers Anthology)
Read more at https://shop.reggibroach.com/.

About the Publisher

Defender Christian Publications is a small press dedicated to helping Christian writers publish their stories. For more information contact Ron Broach at Ron@RBEnterprises.info

www.ingramcontent.com/pod-product-compliance
Lightning Source LLC
LaVergne TN
LVHW090950080826
845145LV00003B/954